QUEST 4

Faith

The Journey to Experience the Phenomenal Marriage That You Deserve

ISBN: (Insert ISBN Number for your Book)

QUEST 4

Faith

The Journey to Experience the Phenomenal
Marriage That You Deserve

QUEST GREEN

Visit www.jquestgreen.com
For marital resources to help you.

CONTENTS

*God, it's me, Quest. I actually am writing the dedication to MY book.
You have given me everything I need in order to complete this and so much
more. I know it's not enough but Thank You.*

*I want to dedicate this book to my family, 'The Green 5.' Faith, you
have been my support system from day one. I am because you are…
To Zoey, Dominic(Nico), and Mason, you are the reason I keep pushing.*

FOREWORD

K nowing Quest for over 25 years, providing he and his wife, Faith, premarital counseling, marrying them in Punta Cana, DR, and then 11 yrs later, renewing their vows in Xcaret, MX, definitely puts me in a position to speak on what kind of "man" Quest is. I've seen him grow exponentially, build his marriage coaching business to what it is today, and become the husband and father I knew he could be. I've seen him at his worst when he was going through a divorce to now. He is happily married and pursuing his passion.

Quest has the experience to be relatable to the couples whom he coaches, and provides them with the tools they need in order to have the phenomenal marriage they deserve. I've seen him speak at conferences and transform couples' lives to help them want and get the help they need. Quest was born to do this. He has a gift to connect with couples and make them feel heard and valued. His commitment in helping them through challenges makes him a great resource for those who want to do "the work."

In my own career and personal life, Quest has been like family. He was there when Dede and I celebrated 25 years of marriage. He was there when I graduated with my PhD, and he has even coached my own son. Quest believes in being present when it matters, and he definitely personifies a "Man of God." I am thrilled to call him a friend, brother, and family.

Dr. Eric Thomas
"ET The Hip Hop Preacher"

FOREWORD

I am excited for you to read this book by my friend, Quest Green. I met Quest at the wedding of our mutual friends, Jarobi and Danielle. Personally, I was going through a very emotional time, so I was excited to have been invited to a moment so filled with love. I was struck by the nowness of his message along with the wedding vows and the way he made us all feel present and at home – in a literal field – loving on our friends. At that point, I was deeply reading every book you could find about love and intimacy. Literally. Every. One. I didn't find anything cohesive about how I was feeling in any single one of them, but in that moment at that wedding and through his words, I understood that there was such a thing as a successful marriage, AND there was absolutely such a thing as a successful friendship. That stuck with me. As I've gotten to know Quest by following his journey, viewing his coaching sessions, and watching him online, I see where the knowledge comes from.

His actual life.

While we are always learning, when it comes to love, the intent is to commit to growth, find our groove, and become friends with it. I believe there is a roadmap in this book.

Estelle
Grammy Award Winning Artist

INTRODUCTION

I promise you, I definitely have lived life! I have been to a number of places, countries, areas, and spaces. I have had numerous life experiences - some wonderful and some not so great. One thing is for sure. There are not many experiences that are as tragic and not only impactful in the present, but generationally destructive like divorce. The ripple effect even after the legal proceedings have ended stretches farther than one would ever think. I know because I not only experienced it but had to deal with the damaging effects YEARS after it happened.

Marriage is a very wonderful and rewarding institution, but it can also feel like a prison if it is not done properly. Too many couples around the world experience this tragedy simply because they want the end result without laying the groundwork. It's quite interesting that in order for divorce to happen, you must be married. However, the ones who marry properly, in other words, and lay the necessary groundwork prior to marriage never see divorce! Divorce is nothing more than the absence of tools and a mindset necessary to navigate through challenges and difficulties present in marriage. You only can achieve that through the process of self-assessment and by making the necessary adjustments on yourself.

I wrote this book with those ideas in mind. If you ever wondered if you were the only one going through these challenges in your marriage, or if you don't know where to start in your marriage, then this book is for you. I was married for 2 years, and then I got divorced. I remarried 7 years later and have been blissfully married for almost 12 years. Through many missteps, mistakes, and adjustments and by rediscovering myself through self-assessment and a number of defining moments and experiences, I have learned what it means to be a consummate husband.

I am a professional marriage coach and author, and I have been blessed to speak to large numbers of people at many marriage conferences. My goal is to help as many people discover their power as a couple and achieve the phenomenal relationship that they and so many marriages deserve. I have my own marital community called *The Greenhouse Marriage Community* where we teach how to embrace the proper mindset necessary to navigate through the difficulties, challenges, and opposition that marriage can present.

Every day is a new day and a new opportunity to serve Faith (my wife) in a way I have never served her before. I zeroed in on 4 areas that keep me accountable as an individual, so I can be the husband, father to our children, and friend she always wanted. Those areas are FOUNDATION, LOVE, LIFESTYLE and LEGACY. I have been on that journey for the last 12 years, and I am just getting started. It is indeed work, I'll be honest, but the rewards are exponentially more than the journey, and my life is blessed because of it. It's your turn. It's your time. Take the journey!

PART ONE
Foundation

CHAPTER

ONE

FOUNDATION

"And God blessed them and said to them, Be fruitful and multiply and fulfill the earth and have dominion."

Genesis 1:28

M arriage has to be one of the most beautiful institutions that God ever created for a number of reasons that we like and dislike. We love it because of all the pleasantries and all the feel-good vibes that it gives us when we are knee deep in the feeling of love. However, we dislike it when the moments of challenge and difficulty show up. Simply put, we love it when marriage is giving

QUEST GREEN |

what we want to us, but we don't like it when it requires something from us. There are four elements that I'd like to introduce in this chapter that work in conjunction with one another through the idea of what is required in order to have a successful marriage. They are:

1. Marriage
2. Love
3. Commitment
4. Abandoning All Exit Strategies

If you don't remember anything else in this book, remember this… marriage requires love. Love requires commitment, and commitment requires abandoning all exit strategies.

When Faith and I made the decision to be married, we did so because we loved one another, and I'm not talking about the butterflies in the stomach kind of love. That kind of love comes and goes and is not sustainable. I am talking about the kind of love that causes us to be committed to one another in such a way that even when I don't like her, because of true love, I am committed to her and want nothing but the best for her despite the temporary feeling I have of not liking her. We will discuss this more in chapter 6, but sometimes that requires the "best" to come from me in the midst of not liking her. That kind of love is based on a decision and not based on a feeling. I had the opportunity to speak with a friend of mine who happens to be a neurologist, and we were talking about how the brain works, and he said something that blew me away. He said that when a situation arises, or the brain perceives some sort of threat, it originates at the back of the brain. It then passes through the limbic

20 |

system and goes to the frontal lobe where all our decisions are made. He went on to say that our emotions reside in our limbic system, so we actually feel a situation before we actually think about it. Amazing! Additionally, it is a perfect explanation as to why we handle our conflict the way we do. We, in most cases, don't give ourselves an opportunity to think about what has happened before we respond. We feel the situation, and before we think about it, off to left field we go. Our first resolve always should be to – regardless of our feelings – restore harmony. That is not an easy task, but easy has nothing to do with taking ownership and being responsible.

As some of you already know, there are moments in your marital journey when you want nothing to do with your spouse simply because your spouse has gotten on your last nerve or frustrated or angered you in some way. I am sure you realize that you probably have gotten on your spouse's nerves just as much. Maybe you haven't, but if your response is not one that brings restoration to the situation, to your spouse, and/or to your marriage then you need to make some adjustments as well. It may not be your fault, but it is definitely your responsibility. Some of you may be entertaining thoughts of separation or divorce. However, I caution against having those thoughts simply for the fact that wherever your mind goes, your energy flows. It will not be long before what you entertain in your heart becomes reality. Once again, I caution you and encourage you to think differently as it relates to challenges in your marriage. Abandon the thought of doing life without your spouse. Remember that you made a commitment, and that commitment should remind you that you did it for love. You either asked or accepted to do life with your spouse, and this principle is foundational to marriage. I would like to add the disclaimer that abuse is very real and I am not an advocate for entertaining abuse in any of its forms. If that is a factor, then you have every right to protect yourself and your children - if you have any - even to the extent of leaving. However if that is not a factor then please be very thoughtful in the thoughts you entertain.

It is amazing to me that of all the things God could have said after putting the first marriage together, the first thing he said to them was to be fruitful, multiply, subdue the Earth, and have dominion. I would like to spend a little time on the command to be fruitful because multiplying, subduing, and having dominion cannot happen without fruitfulness. Fruitful is another word for responsibility or being responsible. My daughter came to live with me midway through her freshman year of high school. Her mother and I had been divorced since 2005. Six years later, I was remarried in 2011 to the former Faith Bonilla. Until that time, Zoey spent most of her life with her mom. Of course, she visited on numerous occasions, and she was very familiar with Faith. She absolutely loved her brothers, Nico and Mason, but in hindsight, I know the transition must have been a difficult one for her. Truth be told, there were moments when it was difficult for Faith and me. It's amazing that after achieving growth and arriving at particular milestones in my journey, there were still moments when because of feelings, I made Zoey's transition more about me and less about her. Growth is not growth until it is tested, and your response to the adversity will determine whether or not true growth has taken place. I quickly refocused after being reminded by Faith that we wanted her to be with us because we knew that it would be much better for her to be here. Faith said, "We will be to her what we said we will be to her. We will love and provide structure no matter what the situation is." That caused me to start looking at Faith in a whole new light. She now was exhibiting the attributes of "covenant" and not a contractual relationship. Covenant relationships are those of the mindset that say, "Nothing will separate me from you." Contractual relationships are those bound only by signature, and as soon as that contract has expired, or things go south, so does the relationship. Faith had purposed in her heart and mind that she was going to live in a covenant, and later, she would show it through her actions and not just in her speech.

It was never my intent to have a blended family, but that's exactly what I had, and I had to learn quickly how to navigate through all the different dynamics associated with having one. If you know anything about having to learn how to navigate through difficult family dynamics quickly, then you know that YOU WILL make a mess a number of times. However, no matter how big of a mess I would make, because I was committed, I would clean up the mess every time. I would make the apologies as difficult as they would be and have the challenging conversations necessary to bring closure to negative experiences within the family.

Zoey finally got it together during her junior year of high school, but let's just say during that transitionary period, her behavior was less than desirable. Faith and I were challenged on a number of fronts with her behavior. I don't know about Faith, but I was tempted to send her back to her mother. Of course, I knew I could never send her back, and I quickly had to divorce the idea because it was indeed not in alignment with the fruitful vision we said we wanted for our family. We had countless discussions, many trips to her high school to meet with administrators about misconduct at school, and moments when I raised my voice in frustration because of her behavior, but I tried my best to maintain structure and some level of order to everything I did with her.

Faith would love on her in so many ways, but she gave her a strong rebuke when she needed it as well. Where Faith had the upper hand as it related to Zoey was with their relationship. What made Zoey able to receive the rebuke was that same relationship. Zoey realized that Faith loved me, and because she(Zoey) was a part of me, she realized that Faith loved her as well. Faith wanted nothing but the best for her, regardless of her behavior, and even in the face of adversity, she showed it. Although she showed her love verbally, Faith demonstrated her love for Zoey through her actions.

Faith would do things like have lunches with her. If Faith was going to get her nails done, she would take Zoey with her. She would have conversations about boys with her. It was literally amazing to watch. I must add though that Zoey knew Faith from the time we started dating, which was somewhere towards the end of the summer of 2009, so it was indeed foundational to where they were in terms of their relationship.

What Faith was doing was being fruitful. In other words, she was operating with responsibility. Me? Not so much. My parents are from Jamaica, W.I., and I grew up under the mindset that children are to be seen and not heard. I felt that Zoey was supposed to do as I said and not as I did. That, unfortunately, was the mindset under which I was working. I come from a place and time where you did what your parents said to do, or you simply "suffered the consequences." What

I now realize, is that may have worked in Jamaica or when you were growing up, but the truth is we are not in Jamaica, and these are definitely different times. I learned that through watching Faith operate with our daughter. More than anything, I realized that my no tolerance mindset, while appropriate for attacking life and business goals, was not conducive necessarily for my relationship with Zoey. I quickly made the adjustments and began speaking differently to Zoey. Don't judge us, but we LOVE the Waffle House. I implemented what I call Daddy and Zoey time when we would go and have conversations over a cheese omelet and waffles.

Through our relationship building, there was one thing that I said to her that I believed caused her to start thinking differently about her situation and the place where she was in her life. She would want to go to numerous places with her friends, do numerous things, and take part in numerous activities, but I would tell her no on many occasions because of her track record associated with her behavior. It became a frustrating thing for her as well because she wanted to go to all these places, and I honestly wanted her to enjoy being a teenager and experience the fullness of that season of her life, but because of the track record of her behavior, I would not allow her to go. Of course, Faith would operate as Zoey's advocate and always give me the perspective of not having her father in her life. She would tell me that I can't hold on to Zoey forever. Essentially, Faith was giving me "game" on the development of my daughter and the things I needed to do to form a bond with her, but it was also the catalyst for a deeper bond between Faith and me.

I remember saying to Zoey countless times that freedom is a byproduct of responsibility. I told her, "If you want to go to these places with your friends, then you are going to have to show responsibility and not just for the here and now. It is going to have to be a lifestyle for you, so you establish a new track record. I want to be able to trust that you know how to conduct yourself and how to behave, and once you are responsible, then you will get more freedom." I said it to her until I was blue in the face. I drilled it into her head so many times that when I began to say it, she would finish the sentence for me by saying, "Yes, Daddy, I know...it's a byproduct of responsibility." It wasn't until her junior year that some of her friends started to drive, specifically her best friend Zoe. I know some of you might be confused, but Zoey and her best friend have the same name - Z and Z as they like to call themselves. She was really an answer to prayer. Now, Zoe (her best friend) was a year ahead of her in high school. Her Mom worked with Faith, so that was an added bonus. She was extremely responsible. She got excellent grades, and she was well behaved, so anywhere that my Zoey wanted to go with Zoe (her best friend), I approved. However, there were some other friends with whom she wanted to go out on occasion, and I didn't know them or their parents, and in connection with her track record, my answer was always no. Zoey definitely was paying attention.

Sidebar, you are the sum total of the people with whom you associate. Miss Vernessa - Dr. Eric Thomas's Mom - always used to say, "You hang around nine broke people, you are bound to be the tenth." That's how influence works, so as I stated earlier, my Zoey wanted her own car as well. She would say to me, "Daddy, I think it's time for me to learn how to drive." My response to her once again would be, "No." Why? I felt that if I put her behind the wheel of a car with her track record in connection with responsibility, the chances were that she might kill somebody, and more importantly, she might kill herself.

How you do one thing is how you do everything. If you respond irresponsibly in one area, chances are you'll be irresponsible in multiple areas. There's no telling what you would do behind the wheel of a car while driving - texting, looking where you're not supposed to be looking, or not focusing on the road. In other words, being irresponsible could result in killing yourself, not to mention other people along with you.

Just before graduating high school, something happened. It was almost as if somebody turned a light switch on, and she made a complete 180-degree turn. It was as if she had an epiphany! Maybe she did, but I think she began to see that her behavior was not working for her. It was working against her. I believe in her own way, she started to realize that she was losing out on life because of her decisions, and she started not only making the adjustments, but also she started making better decisions. Faith and I had another discussion, and she reminded me that if Zoey was making adjustments, so should we. I agreed, and Faith started teaching her how to drive. It was a major thing for me to swallow, but once again, the objective was to be fruitful. If Zoey was being fruitful, then so should we.

CHAPTER

TWO

FOUNDATION PART II

Z oey and I have a podcast together called "Zoey's Got a Dad" on Apple podcast platforms. Through our many discussions on that podcast, we'd revisit the times when she was not as responsible as she should have been. She specifically talked about how it felt losing in so many areas of life, time and time again because of her decisions and lack of responsibility. It really was nothing less than extraordinary. She understood that one of the first things that she needed to do in order to win and start living life was to be responsible. The first thing that she did was get a job, and in addition to that, she started saving money.

While she was saving money, we had many discussions about her driving.

She started showing many different areas of responsibility and because of that, I started to allow her to go to different places with her friends. I allowed her to stay out a little bit later than normal because she continued to show that she could be responsible, not to mention she liked how her new freedom felt. She would always come home at curfew, and if she was running a couple of minutes late, she would always call and let me know she was on her way. That freedom that she started to experience was a byproduct of her exhibiting responsibility. I am proud to say that Zoey has now completed her first year of college and is about to enter into her second year of college. She saved up and bought her own car, and she is literally "Livin' La Vida Loca." She still calls and checks in no matter what she is doing, and she realizes the power of responsibility.

There are many who understand the Biblical mandate, "Be fruitful, multiply, subdue the Earth and have dominion," but they never can accomplish the first step of the mandate, simply because they lack responsibility! The kind of fruitfulness(freedom) that we desire in our marriages and in our lives cannot be accomplished without a consistent effort, and an effort that is rooted in responsibility. No one is going to drop fruitfulness in your lap. It requires a mindset! One that says "I will show up and execute in a manner that is in alignment with my commitment to my marriage despite my feelings. There are many couples who are not experiencing the best that marriage has to offer simply because they talk recklessly to one another. They don't meet each other's needs unless their needs are being met. They hold their spouses hostage to expectations, while denying or being defensive behind their own faults. These are behaviors that are highly irresponsible.

Because of the decisions that Faith and I made together to be fruitful, responsible, and committed despite what we often felt, Zoey is thriving, and our marriage is that much stronger because of it. If you want to experience a newness in your marriage, start looking at the areas in which you are irresponsible. How do you talk to one another? Are you a man or woman of your word? What do your conversations consist of? When you go out with friends, do you come back at a reasonable time? How do you make your decisions? Do you make them without considering your spouse? Wives, do you handle your husband with respect? Husbands, do you handle your wife with love? The word, fruitful, as I stated earlier, can be understood as responsibility, and it is the very institution that God holds with high esteem. He has blessed you and your spouse with the ability to be fruitful, and that must be treated with responsibility.

Some of you want the freedom to have a wonderful relationship. Some of you want the freedom to have good communication in your relationship. Some of you want the freedom that trust provides in your relationship. Some of you want the freedom that connection - emotional, physical, and/or spiritual - provides in your relationship. However, the truth of the matter is you are not responsible in your actions as it relates to your spouse. Marriage is not only for the purposes of coexisting or cohabitating. It is for both of you to be fruitful. I know we said that fruitfulness means responsibility, but fruitfulness also means to build something, right? It means building something together, and that requires you to have a mindset that facilitates fruitfulness.

When we look at the parable of the talents found in Matthew 25, we see a master going away on a long trip. He gave one servant five talents. He gave another servant two talents, and he gave another servant one talent. The servant who had five talents turned them into ten talents. The servant who had two talents turned them into four talents. However, the last servant did nothing with his talent. As a matter of fact, he hid it in the ground.

Upon the master's return, they all presented what they had done with the talents he gave them. To the first two servants, the master responded and said, "Well done thou good and faithful servant. You have been faithful over a few, and now I will make you ruler over many." CATCH THAT! Because they had been responsible with what they received from the master, he gave them a whole lot more. Some of us want a whole lot more, but we lack the responsibility that garners "a whole lot more." It was the master's response to the last servant who hid his talent in the ground that shook me. The master's response was, "You wicked, lazy, and slothful servant. Off into utter darkness with you where there will be weeping and wailing and gnashing of teeth." Now, I thought this response was a bit harsh, but this demonstrates that God is serious about what He has blessed you and how responsible you should be with what He has given you.

The truth is that the last servant was blessed with a gift. He was blessed with a talent, and he did nothing with it. Can I share with you that marriage is a gift, and it must be cultivated? It must be taken care of. It must be handled with responsibility. I don't know about you, but a place where there is darkness, weeping, and wailing and gnashing of teeth does not sound like a place that I want to visit.

That is what happens in our marriages when we don't cultivate what God has given us. Marriage is not a promise or something to which you are entitled. It is a privilege to be a part of this institution, and if we do not treat it accordingly, difficulty, challenges, opposition, frustration, and anger always seems to be the end result. When God placed Adam and Eve in the Garden of Eden, He told them to take care of it, build it up, and tend to it. In other words, what He was teaching them was responsibility. The garden was their responsibility. The only thing that God told him not to do was to eat from the Tree of Knowledge of Good and Evil. Truth be told, they did absolutely well until Eve was approached by the serpent. I love how Dr. Myles Munroe lays it out through his philosophy of vision. His philosophy states that when you've been given vision, anything that you're about to do, any decision that you're about to make, any thought that you have, and any action that you're about to carry out that is not in alignment with the vision should not be done.

I have come to realize that because we have a certain understanding and because most of us have a decent grasp on the difference between right and wrong, the devil never really tries to get us to do anything bad because he knows that we're not going to do it. However, what he does try to do is get us to do things that are good. In other words, he wants us to do things that are not necessarily in alignment with the vision. Just because something is good, does not mean that it is right or in alignment with the vision. If it's not good, then it shouldn't be done. However if it's good, but it's not in alignment with the vision, it serves as a distraction. Remember what Adam and Eve's responsibility was. Remember what they were supposed to do. God told them to take care of the garden and cultivate it, but the serpent came as a distraction. She saw that the fruit was good for consumption - NOT RIGHT FOR CONSUMPTION - so she ate it. She made a decision that was not in alignment with the vision, and we are dealing with the results of that decision to this very day. Fruitfulness and responsibility are disrupted by distraction. Whenever you find yourself being unfruitful, it is because you have allowed yourself to be distracted by someone or something, and that is irresponsible. Vision is very important in marriage because it determines a specific goal you are trying to achieve. Once you've locked in on what the vision is and what you are doing good or bad is not in alignment with that vision, then you are distracted.

What Faith and I have learned is that regardless of the difficulties we face, we face them together. It is not the difficulty that comes at you, it is how you face the difficulty that comes at you. We both love each other, even when we don't like each other, because we are committed to each other, and if you embody that, then any attempt or sentiment for an exit is not an option.

CHAPTER
THREE

KNOW THE CREATOR OF MARRIAGE

"Commit your actions to the Lord and your plans will succeed."

Proverbs 16:3

It is important to not only know who the creator of marriage is, but you must be in a relationship with Him. My first marriage ended in divorce for the following three reasons: 1. I had no business being married because I was not ready for what marriage required of me. 2. I fooled myself into thinking I was in a relationship with the Creator. 3. I made the most important decision I ever would make without counsel. It was all based on feeling and surface attributes. In other words - if I can be transparent - she was 36-24-38, and I was blind to anything else other than what my eyes were taking in. I was immature. I made long-term decisions based on short term information. The chemistry was super strong; however, the compatibility was almost non-existent. I am not saying that compatibility is the end all be all, but it is definitely foundational to agreeing to continue to learn about each other throughout our years of evolution. What complicated things was that we were sexually active long before we decided to get married, which is a huge no no. I know that is probably an unpopular mindset in today's society, but sex before marriage will complicate any relationship not bound by marriage. It secretly clouds your decision-making abilities simply because you don't want to mess up your sexual activity. I'll put it this way, sex is the fire, and marriage is the fireplace. If you start that fire anywhere else, the potential is great to burn the whole place down, and some often do by destroying relationships when the breakup happens, leaving behind broken hearts and collateral damage.

Here's a strange dynamic that exists in marriage. As I said, I had no business being married because I was not ready for what marriage required of me. What is so crazy about marriage is that it requires a version of you that you currently are not. In essence, you are being trained through trial and error on what to do and what not to do, and as soon as you figure out what to do and become a master at it, the goal moves because you're evolving and changing as an individual. In other words, the goal is no longer the same, and growth is taking place, but that is what marriage sets out to do from the very beginning. Remember, the goal is always to be responsible. To build something requires a certain mindset. For many marriages, that mindset is not present, and the only time you find that out is when difficulty arises.

Who will you be when the difficulties of marriage hit? Here's a better question. Who prepares you for the difficulties of marriage when they hit? I thought that just because I was going to church every weekend, because I knew a Bible verse here and there and knew how to apply it, and because I was raised in Christian education, I was ready for marriage or ready for the likes of marriage. I fooled myself into thinking I was in a relationship with God. Truthfully, all I was doing was going through the motions. My life Monday through Friday did not mirror my life in church on Saturday. It's amazing how we as Christians can raise hell during the week and think we are doing okay because we attended church service on the weekend like we're fulfilling some kind of quota. What I have come to realize is that if you are going to talk the talk, you better walk the walk. Life has a funny way of coming to check you or check the authenticity of who you say you are. If you say you're a husband or if you say you're a wife, don't worry because life will be coming with the right recipe to test the authenticity of who you say you are in terms of being a husband or a wife, and when that test comes, who will you be? How will you respond? In marriage as well as in life, it's not what you face. It's how you face it. Look at the story of Abraham and Isaac in Genesis 22 and take into consideration the fact that the marital relationship is indeed a mirrored representation of our relationship with God. Abraham was told by God that he would be the father of nations, and he was told that he would be considered the father of faith because of his relationship and obedience to God.

How you face marriage and its difficulties is determined by how you are prepared, and how you are prepared is by knowing the Creator. Let me be very clear, marriage will take you to some places where what you think, what you drive, where you live, who you know, how much money you have, and what you think you know about relationships can't and won't help you. The only thing that will be able to get you through those moments will be your relationship with God and your obedience to His commands.

It's imperative that you not only know the Creator of marriage, but you must establish a relationship with Him. It's imperative that you know His voice. It's imperative that you don't do life around God, but you must do life with God. When the marriage relationship gets difficult and causes you to be mentally strained, frustrated, and downright angry, you need to be able to hear the voice of God and understand how to respond. Remember what I said? It's not what happens in marriage. It's how you respond to what happens in marriage. Being in relationship with the Creator and being able to hear His voice when He speaks when those challenges push you is priceless. These are the moments when you need to pull from a Source that is unlimited in knowledge, wisdom, and understanding, and the only person I know who is unlimited in those areas specifically is GOD!

However, I am always asked specifically by non-believers, "Are you saying that I cannot have a good marriage unless God is in it?" Absolutely not. However, I am saying who or what is the reference point when you are both entrenched in your thoughts and feelings as it relates to difficulty in opposition in your marriage. Let me be very clear, changed people change people. Your marriage will not change unless you change. Why? God doesn't change situations. He changes people, and people change situations. There is only one person that I know who is able to change people at the core, hence the reason it is imperative to know the Creator of marriage. The truth is some of us need a change in thought, mind, and spirit as it relates to our marital relationship, and if you know that to be you, I would admonish you to get to know the Creator.

WORK:

1. How are you developing your spirit? A sure fire way to make sure that you are developing your spirit daily is to have a devotional time, preferably in the morning. If you are just starting, spend roughly 15 minutes reading the bible or some devotional devotional reading and then another 15 minutes meditating on that reading and how it applies to you.

2. When you are perplexed in your marriage, to whom do you go? What is your first resort in attempts to resolve? Make God first in your marriage! Make prayer a major part of your relationship. Keep a good marriage coach if possible join a marriage community.

3. Do you have a relationship with God?

4. If not, what can you do to start one?

CHAPTER

FOUR

WHO DO I NEED TO BE?

"Growth requires becoming..."

Quest Green

There is a wonderful story that my brother, Eric Thomas, tells on YouTube. It has garnered millions of views and is very inspiring. If you have never watched it, and you get the opportunity to view it, you should. It's quite inspiring. It's called "the guru story." He tells the story of a young man who wants to make a lot of money. He goes to see the guru in order to find out how to make this money. When he gets there, he tells the guru what his desire is, and the guru says, "Okay, cool. You want to make money? Meet me out at the beach tomorrow morning at 4:00a.m." The young man thinks to himself, *The beach? I don't want to learn how to swim, I want to learn how to make money.* Nevertheless, the young man shows up at the beach the following morning at 4:00a.m.

When he gets there, the guru is already out in the water. The young man shows up in a suit, and truth be told, he should have worn swim trunks. The guru tells him to come out in the water, and the young man rolls his pants up to his knee and proceeds to walk out into the water. As he's standing in the water, the guru tells him to come out some more to the point where the water is now at his waist. The young man is frustrated at this point and says, "I'm leaving. I didn't come out here to become a lifeguard. I came out here to learn how to make money." As the young man is leaving, the guru yells back at him, "I thought you said you wanted to make money." He tells the young man to come out even deeper. Frustrated and feeling like he wants to leave the beach, the young man goes deeper into the water to the point where the water is now at shoulder level. The young man is now in close proximity to the guru, and the guru grabs him, pushes his head into the water, and holds him underwater. The young man is thrashing. The water is splashing all over the place, and he holds him down under the water for a short amount of time. He finally brings the young man up as he is gasping for air. The young man still is taking long, heavy breaths, and the guru asks him, "What was the one thing you wanted to do when you were underwater?" The young man, barely catching his breath, replied, "I wanted to breathe." The guru responds by saying, "Excellent. When you want to succeed as badly as you want to breathe, then you'll be successful."

The story suggests that there is someone whom the young man had to become in order to be successful at making money. I'm not just talking about the physical act of working or having a job. I'm talking about mind, body, and spirit. There is somebody who you need to become as it relates to your mind, body, and spirit to achieve the levels of success that we're discussing, or that this young man desired.

There may be some classes that he needs to take, a particular school that he needs to attend, or money trends that he needs to study. More importantly than all that, he may need to maintain a particular mindset when trends are not looking the way that they should. He needs to learn how to remain calm in complex situations. Whomever or whatever the goal requires him to be, he needs to become that person in order to make the money he wants. I find it interesting, however, that there are a lot of people who want to be successful, but they do not want to become the individual they need to be in order to become successful. As I stated in chapter one, there are those who want freedom without responsibility. They want the freedom to be successful, the freedom to make money, and the freedom to live how they want to live and drive what they want to drive, but they don't want to be responsible for the work that is associated with that freedom.

Anything worth having is worth going through something to receive, so the pertinent question remains, "Who do I need to be?" It's no different in marriage. The marital relationship is one with a lifelong commitment, and you can't just stumble upon a phenomenal marriage. At the end of most of my marital videos on YouTube, I close the videos by saying "From shaky to good and from good to great, ultimately, what we want is a phenomenal marriage, but phenomenal marriages don't just happen, they take work." Plainly put, phenomenal marriages take work! There are some people who have been married for a year, five years, 10 years, 15 years, and they never have asked themselves, "Who do I need to be for my marriage?"

When was the last time you read a book on marriage or attended a marriage conference? When was the last time you went to a marriage retreat? When was the last time you went to marriage counseling or a coaching session? Therapy perhaps? I just like to add that just because you're not experiencing problems or issues does not negate the importance of seeing a marriage coach or counselor. Faith and I have a marriage coach who we see from time to time not because we're going through anything but simply for the purposes of maintenance. Just imagine driving your car for 5000, 10,000, 15,000, miles and never changing the oil. Of course, you wouldn't do that, or at least I hope you wouldn't. However, the truth is if you did, viscosity would build up. There would be a buildup of sludge. You would have metal on metal in the engine, and it eventually would blow up. When that happens, it's time for a new engine or a new car. The point I'm making is that you change your oil for the maintenance of your car, so it will run efficiently. This was a HARD lesson that I learned as a result of my first marriage. I had no premarital coaching, and during the marriage, even though it only lasted two years, I never read a book, never saw a coach, and never attended a conference. When things began to build up in our marriage, the friction was serious, and as expected, with no tools to navigate the challenges, the end result was the marriage ending in divorce.

Can I be honest? The reason I had no business in marriage the first time I did it wasn't because I wasn't good enough for marriage. It was because I was not aware of who I needed to be for marriage. Marriage is not operated by some mystical force or some random spirit. Your marriage is operated by you as an individual. You've heard the saying, "A chain is only as strong as its weakest link." Well, the same is true of marriage. Your marriage is only as strong as its least developed individual. Marriage always requires a version of yourself that you currently are not. Therefore, the mindset of a student and not that of a finished product is one that definitely should be embraced. Marriage is a learning institution that you enter, but you never graduate from it.

It is very important in your marital relationship that you embrace the mindset of a student with the diligence of a practitioner. As you learn, you execute. Don't only pay attention to the areas in which you are great. Those are the areas where you probably could execute with your eyes closed. Acknowledge the areas where you know you are not great and get reps. In other words, continue to work on those weak areas until they become strong areas.

I have had the opportunity numerous times to walk the illustrious campus of Oakwood University in Huntsville, Alabama. I especially love being there for Alumni Weekend during Easter, but more than the gorgeous campus and the beautiful people that work and attend classes there, there is a mission which is displayed upon entering and leaving the campus. When entering the campus, the marquee says, "ENTER TO LEARN," and upon leaving the campus, it says, "DEPART TO SERVE." What we learn in marriage from situations and our spouses helps us make the necessary adjustments to not only serve but also to become much more developed as spouses.

When I started working from home, I would spend countless hours in my office to the point where I was neglecting time with my wife and children. I thought I was doing the right thing by staying on my grind and trying to build something for my family. There were moments of major difficulty when I was trying to "put the pieces together." No matter how stuck I would get and no matter how drained I was, there would be times when I almost would miss a coaching session because of how tunnel visioned I was. Instead of taking a break, I would just sit there breaking my brain and trying to figure out the next move. When Faith had finally had enough, she asked, "Can we talk?" Of course, I said yes, but the tone hinted that this was not going to be a cake walk conversation. As the conversation began, she wasted no time in explaining to me that I was spending too much time in the office, and it felt like I was cheating on her with our company. She explained that she and the children needed my time as well. I will admit there was a part of me that wanted to buck and say, "Here is another opportunity for her to tell me how bad my time management is." Just as I thought it, she said, "We are not getting the time we need because of your inability to manage your time properly." GREAT! I will admit that what she said was not a lie. I did need to improve my time management skills, I just didn't want to be told about it. As I felt the need to be defensive, I heard the Holy Ghost say, "Sit there. Don't say a word and listen to what she's saying."

What was being revealed to me was the truth. No matter how I felt about it. It didn't matter that I was experiencing a lemon squeeze. The truth is the truth! Now, I had two ways I could have responded to what she said. I could have been defensive and in my feelings about the encounter. I could have been sour and been worse than I was when we started the conversation. However, that outcome would have led to stagnancy in the relationship, a breakdown of trust, and a host of other issues that would have stunted our growth as a couple, or I could have embraced the burn and used it to make the adjustments that would catapult me to the next level of our marriage. I chose to embrace the burn and grow. I responded with, "You're right!" There was an awkward silence for about 2 or 3 seconds. She couldn't believe that I wasn't being defensive. As a matter of fact, she had this confused Scooby Doo look on her face. Her only response was, "How can I help?" I responded by saying, "Since you are the detail oriented one, and you're more structured than I am, can you please come and help me revamp my calendar."

She agreed. As she began to revamp my calendar, she proceeded to do it in 20 minutes, which probably would have taken me an hour and a half to two hours to complete the task.

We now have a schedule for what we like to call our mind body and soul time. That is the time when Faith and I put the kids to bed. We get in bed and we discuss our plans and our future goals. It is a time when we are in our relationship and we address all things related to Quest and Faith. That's our pillow talk time. That same revamped calendar has time for what Nico likes to call "Daddy Nico time" when I spend time solely with him, doing what he wants to do while pouring into him, so he can be all that he needs to be. There is also time for me to chase Mason around the house a little bit, and he is good to go. It keeps Faith feeling secure.

SIDEBAR: Nothing makes a mother happier and more secure in her marriage than to see her husband spend quality time with her children.

Even our 19-year-old, Zoey, has time set aside for us to go to the Waffle House, which is one of her - ok our - favorite places. That time is set aside whether she wants to use it or not. We now have a system in place that allows me to operate efficiently. I love the way my friend, Preech, says it. He says, "Put a system in place to handle your inefficiencies or earn the right to hire someone to do it for you." Our favorite seven words between my wife and me now are, "Did you put it on the calendar?"

I literally put everything on my calendar from things that I need to remind myself to do to all the honey-do items including things that she's asked me to do, and guess what. My time management is better. She is pleased. There's time for the kids and time for her, and harmony is restored. Remember what I said. You must embrace the mindset of a student with the diligence of a practitioner. You must be able to learn from your spouse and situations. What worked last season in your marriage won't necessarily work now. As you learn, simply execute. The hang up for most people is preconceived notions about how a situation is going to turn out, which is reflected in their pride and ego. There are a number of spouses who always feel the need to be right. To those people, I would like to share with you that you are setting yourself up for failure. Unless you are God, NO ONE knows it all. If you did, you wouldn't be reading this book.

Years ago, I embraced the fact that I don't know it all. When you embrace the mindset of a student, it puts you in position for phenomenal growth. Moreover, an "L"(loss) is not an "L" if you learn. Be a student! Learn everything there is to know about your spouse and your marriage even as it evolves and changes through life's seasons. P.R.I.D.E. is Perpetually Repeating Ignorant Decisions Every day. E.G.O. is Etching God Out. Those two acronyms are the antithesis of your marriage. There are many who operate in them, and they lose terribly. Don't let that be said about you.

WORK:

1. Who are you in your marriage? I know that is a loaded question. Seriously, remove the car, the house, your job, and think about who you are as an individual in your marriage. Spend some time developing that individual.
2. How do you balance your time in your marriage?
3. Do you look at difficult moments as opportunities for growth in your relationship?
4. Are you operating, or can you identify when you are operating in P.R.I.D.E. or E.G.O?

CHAPTER FIVE

LAY THE FOUNDATIONS FOR BUILDING

"Build your marriage by design and not by default..."

Quest Green

I am an HGTV addict. I love watching "Fixer Upper" specifically, but I love any show where before they purchase the property, they inspect the home to see where the hidden issues are. I've watched tons of episodes when home adjusters or inspectors come and show the results of a bad foundation. It literally can cause a house to come tumbling down like a house of cards. Some of the homes have cracks in the walls, bows in the floors, sinking and leaning issues, which are all indications of a bad foundation, and if the necessary repairs are not made, after a time, the house will no longer be able habitable, and the cost to make those kinds of repairs most times is astronomical. Sometimes, people purchase properties sight unseen, and then when it is time to do the renovation work, they are overwhelmed thinking, *What did I do? What did I get myself into?* They are overwhelmed because they did not do the pre-work.

Just think about it. Imagine you are a real estate investor, and you see a fixer upper home for $40,000. You call the real estate agent and make an offer for $30,000, and they accept! You're thinking to yourself, *Wow, what a deal.* You have a $120,000 budget, and now that you've purchased the home, you have $90,000 left. You walk into the home with your contractor, and he starts looking around, and you start explaining to him all the different things that you want to do inside this home for the renovation. He responds by telling you after calculating all the expenses that it will cost roughly about $80,000 to complete. You're thinking to yourself, *This is awesome!* You also still have a $10,000 cushion in case of incidentals. However, he walks into another room and sees a long crack in the wall going up to the ceiling.

He looks down, and there's major sinking in the floor, so he decides to go outside and look at the foundation. He sees multiple red flags as it relates to the foundation. After assessing all the issues with the foundation, he says to you that it's going to cost another $60,000 in order to fix the foundation. Your renovation budget now has been blown away. You have a couple of options. 1. You could just walk away from the project, but that won't work because you would be throwing $30,000 away. 2. You could sell it for the purchase price, but how long will that take? The agent gave no resistance at 10k less than asking price, and the seller probably knew about the foundation issues before they sold it. 3. You could take out a loan for the $60,000 and recoup it on the back end by just selling the property once the repairs have been made. I don't know about you, but I would probably go with option 3. Lesson well learned? Absolutely! It is a very costly lesson, but if you learn it, then it is definitely not a loss.

What am I saying? You CANNOT receive beyond your strategy. You must plan! Have conversations about how the next year will look and how the next 5, 10, 15 years will look. Just imagine what next year will produce if you put a marital growth plan in place for you and your spouse. Remember the motto, "We build our marriage by design and not by default." It is not something cute we say. You must believe and execute. Your decision to be married is the most important decision you will make in your entire life. When my brother, Eric Thomas, did premarital coaching for Faith and me, he always would say, "Begin with the end in mind." Declare where you want your marriage to be. Lay out a strategic plan together and work towards the destination. You WILL NOT just cruise through the journey of marriage and get the things that your heart desires for your relationship. YOU. MUST. PLAN!

The major difference between my first marriage and my second marriage was that I learned in my second marriage to build with a lot of intentionality. I was very deliberate. I was deliberate about the way that I thought, the way that I acted, and my response to situations. I made sure that I thought more as it related to my decisions and leaned less on my emotions and my feelings about the situation.

In my first marriage, I was attracted to all the external attributes. I was concerned about how we looked together, how she made me feel, and how exciting the sex was. The good times that we had, all of which were nice, were not sustainable for the likes of marriage. I'm not saying that I am not still attracted to those things, Faith is absolutely gorgeous, but they didn't drive my decision to marry her. When things got bad in my first marriage, they got really bad, and when things get really bad, what you have, how you look, how bomb the sex is, what the chemistry is, and what the surface attributes are can do nothing for you. There is only so much you can endure when you do not have the tools necessary to navigate the challenges and difficulties that marriage can and will present.

Prior to my second marriage, I did the work. I realized that the issues in relationships are never one sided, and when it comes to growth and development, the only person you can control is yourself, so I began to read books in efforts to grow. I remember coming across a quote by Roy Disney that said, "It's not hard to make decisions when you know what your values are." As I dive more deeply into this idea of values, I found out what it meant to have core values. If I had to define core values, I would have to define them as the fundamental beliefs of a person that dictate behavior and can help the person understand the difference between right and wrong. Core values also help people determine if they're on the right path of fulfilling their goals by creating an unwavering guide. That's exactly what I needed - an unwavering guide that would help me make better decisions. From the very start of my second marriage, Faith and I would have discussions about philosophies, ideas, mindsets, principles, and practices that we fully embraced and were not willing to compromise on. Anytime that we would do anything that was not in alignment with what we wanted in terms of those values, we would throw it overboard.

When doing the work that marriage requires, concentrate on cultivating the mindset and attributes that allow you to build a rock-solid marriage. The same way an inspector looks for the issues on a property, self-assess and examine your marriage. Look for the philosophies, ideas, mindsets, principles, and practices in which you currently operate, and if they are not in alignment with what you want in terms of an outcome, then stop operating in them. Make the adjustments necessary. It may require a time and even a money investment, but the returns are so much more than any investment you make.

WORK:

1. What short-term or long-term strategies have you put in place for your marriage?
2. If marriage is only as strong as its least developed individual. How are you working on yourself for the betterment of your marriage?
3. What are your core values? What is your unwavering guide that helps you make your decisions?

PART TWO

Love

CHAPTER

SIX

LOVE

"Love, so many people use your name in vain. Love, those who have faith in you sometimes go astray. Love, through all the ups and downs of joy and hurt. Love, for better or worse, I still will choose you first."

Musiq Soulchild

I want to start this chapter off by simply celebrating love. I simply love the euphoric feelings that love produces. I celebrate the feeling of security you feel when your husband holds your hand in public places, of course, if you're okay with PDA. Ladies, I celebrate the feeling you have when he reaches for your hand while driving in the car. Guys, I celebrate the way she uses her femininity to draw you more deeply into her love and respect for you. I also celebrate the way you both connect when you hear your favorite love song that causes you to say, "That's our song."

During many of my coaching sessions, I spend a lot of time dealing with the difficulties, the challenges, and the opposition of marriage because the good is good, right? You won't hear people complaining about how good a marriage is. However, let's be honest. We do need to take time to celebrate the pleasantries of marriage. It's the thing that keeps the fire burning. It's the thing that in the face of difficulty and challenge allows you to say, "You know what. While things may be bad, there are moments when things are absolutely great, so I wanted to just spend a little time celebrating this part of the relationship because I think it's very important. Too many people are engulfed in the monotony of making business plans, paying bills, taking children to their numerous activities, and wearing all the different hats of life more than they wear the husband and wife hats.

I had a conversation with Inky Johnson a couple of years ago, and we were just talking about the burnout that we at times experience in our careers, and he said something extremely profound. He said, "Quest, people don't get burned out because of what they do. People get burned out because life makes them forget why they did it in the first place." WOW! Inky always waxes deep, but those words were especially heavy. Why? It's not that you don't love each other, or you don't want to spend time with one another. It's that you have allowed the travails of life to pull and push you in so many directions that you have forgotten why you said "I DO" in the first place. The Word declares in Ecclesiastes 3:1, "There is a time and place for everything under the sun." Now, while we all know that marriage is indeed the breeding ground for growth and a number of difficulties and challenges, it is also a place where we can laugh, enjoy the love, and lose ourselves in all that "grown folk" energy has to offer. Trust me. There will be plenty of time for bills, household responsibilities, and all the different things that go into making a home, but I just want to give you a little food for thought. If you do not find time to pour into the love of your relationship, you won't have to worry about "household responsibilities" because you won't have a marriage in which to do it. Am I clear?

Please allow me to ask you a couple of questions. Usually I will wait until the end of the chapter to give you the work portion, but this looks like a perfect place to insert them.

WORK:

1. When was the last time you took her out? Taking her out doesn't necessarily mean an expensive night on the town. Taking her out can mean a picnic, going out for some ice cream, or having a lunch date, etc.
2. Ladies, when was the last time you put on something sexy for him? I want to hip you to the fact that men are very visual creatures. You'd be surprised what you can accomplish by being sexy for him. He may front like he didn't see it, but trust me, he sees!

3. When was the last time you had sex? For the record, sex was made for us to enjoy it.
4. When was the last time you spoke each other's love language in a real and practical way?

Really sit and ask yourself these questions, and if you haven't invested in your relationship, now is the time. When you execute in these areas, you are in essence making an investment/deposit in each other, but more importantly, you are investing in the marriage. Has your love been speaking in a way that your spouse feels and understands it?

I have developed a crucial understanding as it relates to marriage. I believe that marriage requires love. Love requires commitment, and commitment requires abandoning all exit strategies. However, it all starts with love. I cannot stress enough how important it is to make the investment while enjoying the marriage because there will be days when you will have to make a withdrawal, and you cannot make a withdrawal from something in which you never invested. MAKE. TIME. FOR LOVE!

CHAPTER
SEVEN

LOVE DON'T ALWAYS FEEL GOOD

"Love bears all things, believes all things, hopes all things, endures all things. Love never fails…"

1 Corinthians 13:7-8

The kind of love that marriage requires is an unconditional one fueled by humility, vulnerability, maturity, and forgiveness. The truth of the matter is that while we are experiencing all the pleasantries of love and marriage, there will be moments when you don't see eye to eye.

As a matter of fact, there will be times when you are absolutely angry with one another.

The questions then become, "How will you respond to the situation or your spouse in those moments? Will you allow your anger to dictate your interactions with your spouse, or despite your anger, will you let love rule?" If I literally asked these questions, most people would respond by saying, "Let love rule." However, the truth of the matter is that we understand it only in theory because where the rubber meets the road, we miss the mark every time.

I recently was speaking to a friend of mine who is a neurologist. He is absolutely brilliant! He was explaining to me the system by which we process information in the brain when a situation happens. He lightly explained that when it originates, it happens at the back of the brain, right about where the spinal cord meets the brain. It then passes through the side of our brain in the area where our limbic system resides. Then, it moves from the limbic system to the frontal lobe where all of our decisions are made. Now, this happens really fast, but he said, "What is most amazing as I study the brain even more is that our limbic system is also where our emotions sit," so we legitimately feel a situation before we think about it.

As we continued to converse on a deeper level, I understood more and more why we get into trouble. Speaking within the context of marriage, I realized that every time a situation happens, and it starts at the back of our brain and then moves to our limbic system where our emotions sit, we feel the situation before we take a moment to think about how we're going to respond. A lot of the time, we respond before we think about it. Just think about the last unfruitful interaction you and your spouse had with each other. While you were knee deep in the disagreement, were you looking to understand what was going on? Were you simply trying to get your point across without thinking about what your spouse might have been feeling? While emotions are not a bad thing, they definitely never should be placed in the decision-making seat. Your emotions are there only to be used as an indicator that something is not right and to investigate why you are feeling what you are feeling. Truthfully speaking, your emotions should work for you, not against you. Upon coming to a conclusion, you can respond, not from a place of emotion but from a place of decisiveness.

Now, I know that may sound foreign and even crazy to some. You may even say, "When I'm angry with my spouse, I'm angry, and my spouse just is going to have to deal with it." If this is your response or anything remotely close to it, I will go as far as to say that your problem isn't changing what you do. Your problem is changing how you think. Your philosophy as it relates to your marriage allows you to think that this response, "because you are angry," is an acceptable one. However, whether you realize it or not, it is very damaging to your relationship. Through my personal experiences, knowing that love, true love, must be fueled by those things stated at the top of the chapter, the one thing that must be present, so humility, vulnerability and forgiveness can take place is maturity. We started out the chapter with a quote from 1 Corinthians 13:7-8, but in the 11th verse of that same chapter it states, "When I was a child, I spake as a child I understood as a child and thought as a child, but when I became a man, I put away childish things."

I always thought to myself, *Why would God inspire the Apostle Paul to write these words in the middle of what is obviously a love chapter?* It possesses all this lovely banter about love. What love is and what it is not, and then all of a sudden it says, "When I was a child..." Then, one day, it clicked. You cannot experience the kind of marriage that is rock solid and stands the test of time or the kind of love professed in ageless tales, without the presence of maturity. If I may, I would like to take you back to verse 13 just for a moment. There are three points in the verse that I would like to bring to your attention. The phrases are "spake as a child," "thought as a child," and "understood as a child." These words represent a system by which we communicate thoughts, actions, feelings, mindsets, and a number of other things. The truth is that some of us are adults in an adult institution while we are operating with a childish system. Do you see why maturity must be present? If not, you legitimately can be building up your relationship with one hand and tearing it down with the other hand. The next time you have a moment of difficulty, challenge, or opposition, you will be tempted to hold contempt for one another, criticize one another, be defensive, and deny the very thing that you know you are doing that is counterproductive to your relationship. You will even be tempted to stonewall one another, which is very damaging to any marriage simply because it fosters disconnection. Who will you be in those instances? Immaturity as well as maturity will call you. Which one will you answer? Make love a decision and not a feeling. The chances are greater that you will do the right thing when difficulty, challenge, and opposition show up. It won't be easy, but it will be right, and the rewards are a stronger connection as a result.

Recently, I was coaching a lovely couple through a Zoom session. They had logged in, and they were getting themselves situated. He(the husband) was reminding her(his wife) to bring her materials for the session. She(the wife), feeling flustered because of her not so good day and being a bit overwhelmed because they were running a little late for the session, responded to him by being a bit snappy to the point where he was about to respond, and I looked up at the camera. I immediately called her name and kindly asked her to sit down because it was quite obvious that she was emotionally flooded. I asked her and her husband to look at me and hold each other's hand. I proceeded to ask them to take 7 deep breaths, and by the time they were finished, they were a little more relaxed, and she was able to respond without being snappy. I reassured her that it was ok to take a minute, not only now, but any other time she was running late as long as she communicated it. Remember, feelings never should be put in charge. I am not saying that they are not important, but they never should be put in the decision-making seat. Your feelings should put you in position to examine why you feel the way you do, and after coming to a conclusion, make a decision that is in alignment with what you desire for an outcome. Too many marriages have ended in destruction with multiple casualties for the lack of tools and the proper mindset necessary to navigate those moments when the love doesn't feel good.

WORK:

1. Will you heal for love? Will you solicit the help necessary for that healing?
2. What emotional responses to difficult situations do you exhibit that work against your relationship?
3. Have you declared the outcomes you desire, so your actions are in alignment with your desire?

CHAPTER

EIGHT

WHAT DOES LOVE REQUIRE OF ME?

"To be or not to be... that is the question."

Hamlet written by William Shakespeare

Shakespeare proposes an interesting question in the play, *Hamlet*. "To be or not to be..." If you examine the question, it's as if he dismisses the idea of "can you" or "can't you" and proposes the question "will you" or "won't you"? It is either you are going to be "that" spouse, or you are not. Marriage is an institution that you enter to learn but never graduate. It is one that requires growth. Why? It challenges you like no other relationship challenges you, and you never graduate because you and your spouse never remain the same, or at least you shouldn't. If you are experiencing a shift or a change in your relationship that seems to be long standing, it is probably because what used to work no longer works. What used to look good no longer looks good, and what used to suffice is no longer sufficient. That is simply because the person that you married is not the person to whom you are married. I remember the time I asked Faith to have a conversation with me concerning some things that no longer were working for me. As we began to talk, I stated, "This isn't working anymore." She had a really concerned look on her face like, *What do you mean this isn't working anymore?* Trust me when I tell you that you can't just tell a Puerto Rican woman out of the blue that the relationship is no longer working unless you want a revolution to take place! LOL! I immediately put her concerns to rest by confirming, "I am not saying that this - our relationship - isn't working anymore, but how we do our relationship isn't working anymore." I continued, "Just being your husband or the father to our children no longer will suffice. I want to be your best friend. I want to be the person you come to when you have desires you want to discuss, when you haven't had the best day, or even if you had the best day ever! Whatever it is, I want to be your best friend."

Our mind, body, and soul time, which is a time solely set aside for us to have heart to heart discussions about life, goals, aspirations, etc., is really our pillow talk time. We would discuss the idea of how a best friend looks, so we could be on the same page. What I am sharing with you is that as I grew as an individual and experienced a number of different things including communing with God, attending conferences, reading books, and having the most amazing conversations with some of the most amazing people, who I was when I married Faith was not the person I grew to be in that moment. If you love your spouse, you will work on yourself consistently, so you can give your spouse the very best version of yourself you can. This is the reason why love must be present. If true love - and I am stressing the word, true - is present, no matter how difficult or challenging the relationship gets, you will look past the unpleasant feeling to the necessity of tasks that bring life and even restoration to the marriage. As I previously stated, marriage requires love. Love requires commitment, and commitment requires abandoning all exit strategies. However, there is something else that marriage requires. It requires a version of yourself that you currently are not. Hence, this is the reason why marriage is the breeding ground for growth. You will grow, or the relationship will grow sour. The truth is although you will face countless moments when you will be challenged in your marriage, you must make the adjustments and grow simply because love requires it

In chapter three, I discussed the account of Faith sitting me down in our bedroom for a talk.

Although I was developed in the area of the "clapback," what I wasn't developed in was the area of self-assessment. I already knew because of how she asked me to have the talk, this was not going to be an inviting conversation. As I heard the Holy Spirit say, "Sit down, be quiet, listen, and don't respond until she is done, I was obedient. I won't tell you that I wasn't experiencing the feelings of P.R.I.D.E., E.G.O., frustration, and the need to clapback and be defensive. I, not so simply, remained quiet and refrained from interrupting her. One of the things that I was developing at the time, which I am much better at now, is discipline. There are many of you who keep losing in your relationships because you think you know it all. You have a defensive response for every complaint your spouse has with you, and if the truth be told, you don't have to answer everything.

There are moments when you know what your spouse is saying is true about you, and in those moments, you need to remain quiet and make the adjustments. I realized that what my defensiveness was doing was telling her that although I heard her, I still was going to do that thing that was bothering her. In essence, when we do that, what we are telling our spouse is that their feelings or concerns don't matter. That is definitely NOT what I was trying to convey to her, but that's exactly what I was doing, and I knew it was time to start growing in the area of discipline. Do you remember Ecclesiastes 3? There is a time and place for everything under the sun, and right now was the time to remain quiet and hear her out. It was not the time to clapback or be defensive. In case you didn't know, every time you are defensive to your spouse's concerns, whether you realize it or not, you are chipping away at the strength of trust and intimacy, and if you continue to do that, your spouse will be reluctant to take any concerns to you. Why would your spouse take any concerns to someone who only is going to dismiss the concerns with defensiveness and opposition? When that happens, we create a breach in what should be rock solid.

On the journey to a phenomenal marriage, there will be moments when you don't feel like apologizing. You won't feel like remaining quiet, and you won't feel like operating with discipline and maturity. Some of us simply want to act out like a child, but the facts are that you are not a child, and your feelings have nothing to do with it. Do what is necessary, not what is in your feelings. You may not feel like going to work, but it is necessary that you pay your bills. I am currently on a health journey, and there are days when I show up to the gym and don't feel like working out. However, I declared that I wanted to be healthy, and I meant it. When I show up to the gym, my feelings have nothing to do with the necessity of working out if I want to be healthy. I can hear that word, commitment, ringing in my ear right now. It means doing what you said you were going to do long after the "feeling" you said it in is gone." Might I remind you that YOU said, "I DO," for better or worse, for richer or poorer, and in sickness and health.

Love requires personal development and self-assessment. Remember, your marriage is only as good as its least developed individual. Do you really want to be the weakest link? I have coached a number of couples, and one spouse says about the other, "They never do anything but come home and stare into the phone and scroll for hours." The spouse may say, "All my spouse does is binge watch episodes on Netflix." I am not saying that there's anything wrong with either activity, but the Word declares that there is a time and place for everything under the sun. In other words, balance is the key. Now, some who read this may say, "I just want to scroll through my phone or binge watch my episodes in peace," but I caution you that this mindset is selfish. Marriage and selfishness are polar opposites. I was reading an article from the World Health Organization, and the article stated that sedentary lifestyles increase all causes of mortality rates and double the risk of cardiovascular diseases, diabetes, and obesity, and it increases the risk of colon cancer, high blood pressure and osteoporosis, lipid disorders, depression, and anxiety. Think about that for a moment. All these life-threatening diseases are increased simply because of non-movement or the refusal to do something as simple as take a walk every day.

As I was writing, I looked up the formal definition of sedentary, and it stated it as "a person tending to spend much time seated; displaying inactivity." Too many of us have lived sedentary lifestyles in our marriage, and it is increasing the chances of defensiveness, contempt, criticism, and stonewalling, not to mention a number of other negative attributes. It is affecting our mindset, our self-esteem, and a host of other issues that lead to the one direction in which no marriage should be headed. The one thing that always should be the result of our love for our spouse, as I stated earlier, is being the best version of yourself you can possibly be, and this is accomplished through self-development. It helps enhance your strengths that can be a major asset to your marriage, improve your mental health, and even heal your relationship in some instances. When you read the text found in John 3:16, it states, "For God so loved the world, that HE GAVE..." If God is love, and He loved us so much that He gave His son, so we would have the opportunity to grow in grace and be evidence producers of that fact, what do you think is now our responsibility? Love requires you to give of yourself and your time to your spouse. Read a book with your spouse and have conversations about it. Try something new with your spouse. Take a walk together. Wake up early and have worship or exercise together, just to name a few options. Do it for your growth, so you can be a better asset to your relationship, but more importantly, do it because love requires it.

WORK:

1. What kind of conversation time have you implemented in your marriage to address growth, difficulties, or challenges?
2. Can you identify what your relationship is requiring of you?
3. What uncomfortable areas do you need to face and address, so growth may be facilitated?

CHAPTER

NINE

HOW TO LOVE MY SPOUSE

"How do I love my spouse effectively?"

Many

The question above has to be one of the most common questions posed amongst those who are trying to grow as individuals in their marriages. My mind goes to a text in Luke 6:38 which simply states, "Give, and it shall be given unto you, pressed down, shaken together, and running over with good measure." Notice how the text starts out. If there is one thing I know about God, I know that He is very purposeful. Now, He could have said, "Give at your church. Give at work, or give to your favorite charity, etc." He could have been even more specific and said, "Give of your money. Give of your time. Give of your resources." However, He made a blanket statement and said, "Give." Now, I would like to insert a little piece here at the top of this text, especially for the believer. The word "give," as stated in the text, does not sound like a suggestion. As a matter of fact, it is a command. He is not asking us to give. He is COMMANDING us to give. Give to each other your time, your love, and your thoughts, especially to the needs of your spouse. Give of your body, your conversation, your honesty, your commitment, your integrity, and your character; do you see where I am going with this? If marriage is a reflection of our relationship with God, we should give because HE gave. Let's take a look at what John 3:16 says, shall we? It reads, "For God so loved the world, that he gave his only begotten son that whosoever believeth in Him shall not perish but have everlasting life." Did you see it? For God so loved the world that He GAVE. If you are looking to love your spouse effectively, GIVE! Give your spouse everything you have! Share with them your joys, your finances, your emotions, but don't just share the good things alone. Share your disappointments, your defeats, your sorrows, and your shortcomings with your spouse. I know some may be asking, "Quest, why would we share our not-so-good stuff." I am glad you asked. You also must understand the wiring of both husbands and wives. You share the not-so-good moments because wives always want to be connected to you -good, bad, or indifferent. It allows emotional intimacy to grow between you and her, which is what fuels her love in the relationship. Husbands always want to feel needed, so when you share your "not-so-good" moments, whether they are providing a solution or just lending a listening ear, you fulfill their need to be needed.

Marriage is an institution of benevolence. It is one of service and giving. You must make deposits of everything you have. The institution is also one of withdrawals. In other words, there will come a day when you will need something from the relationship. If you have not withdrawn anything, don't worry. Sit tight. It's coming. If you have no need to withdraw anything from the relationship, then you are not doing marriage correctly. In either case, you cannot make withdrawals on anything if you have not deposited anything into it. When we make withdrawals, as we often will, if you have not deposited anything into it, your effort will be classified as an insufficient attempt to withdraw from something into which you never have invested. That is called stealing! Are you comfortable with stealing from your spouse? I didn't think you would be. Be sure to make deposits in your marriage.

I love the contrast between the wiring of men and women. Women are more likely to move based on their emotional connection to their husbands. Husbands are more likely to move based on their physical connection to their wives. Although the root of the connection is very different, they are very much interdependent on one another. When I'm looking my best, although my wife is pleased that her husband looks good, she is not very impressed. What she is impressed with is when I am vulnerable with her and share my deepest thoughts and feelings. She's impressed when I wash her clothes, fold them up, AND put them in their respective drawers. When I vacuum the carpet and fill her tank up with gas, THEN she is impressed. Half the stuff my wife wants to talk about is really nothing I am interested in personally, and I am not really enthused about having those conversations. However, when she indulges me in the area of "physical connection," and my cup runneth over, she can't get me to shut up about anything she wants to talk about! It is a two-way street of meeting needs and getting your needs met.

As the relationship grows, and you are setting the right foundation, the dynamics change just a little bit. I am in a season of my life with Faith in which those areas of interest that she has that were not so interesting to me and some of them are still not that interesting have become my interests because she is interested in them, and I am interested in her. In Psalms 90, there is a text that says, "Teach us to number our days so that we may apply wisdom to our hearts." That text always hits hard. Why? It reminds us that life is very short. It is a privilege to be married, and it is not a promise. As I get older with my wife, I am starting to appreciate her more and more, and I realize how lucky I am to have her in my life. That's what makes Psalms 90 so real in terms of applying wisdom to our hearts. There are many men that she could have chosen to marry, but she is married to me. I say that not from a low self-esteem standpoint but from one of great appreciation. Some people say that they have to do things for their spouse because they feel that they have to do them. I have reached a point in my life that I understand that I get to do things for my spouse, and I do those things with appreciation and gratitude.

When I spoke of growth in earlier chapters this is the growth I was referencing. It does not matter that she likes or doesn't like what I like. What matters is that I understand there is a sacrificial love that I must extend to her. That means that there will be times when you will have to do things for your spouse that you don't necessarily want to do. Do you only give or do for your spouse only what you want to give or do for them? If so, that is very selfish, and that is a mindset you probably should eliminate immediately. I serve Faith Green, not out of obligation to her and not necessarily out of duty. There are times where I am watching the game, and I don't want to be interrupted, or there are times when I am about to enjoy something that I do for me, and she will ask me to do something for her during that time. Although I don't want to do it, honestly speaking, I will stop and do it anyway because I want to communicate to her not just the feel-good love that I have for her but the sacrificial love I have for her as well. As I stated earlier, I serve her not out of obligation or duty but simply because I love her. In order to love your spouse effectively, you must understand the dynamic of giving and receiving, and it starts with GIVING. Too many marriages have failed because they don't understand this dynamic, or they are simply selfish. In any case, this works counterproductively to the lifestyle and legacy that you want to build.

WORK:

1. In what areas have you failed to "give" to your spouse?
2. Is there anything that prevents you from giving to your spouse?
3. In what ways can you give to or serve your spouse that will allow your spouse to feel your love effectively?

PART THREE

Lifestyle

CHAPTER

TEN

LIFESTYLE

"The greatest glory in living lies not in never falling, but in rising every time we fall."

Nelson Mandela

L ifestyle is defined as, "The typical way of life of an individual, group or culture." Lifestyle is also associated with reflecting or promoting an enhanced or more desired way to live. Now, I know that we all promote and desire marriages that reflect all the goodness that married life has to offer. We want to give and receive coffee from our spouse before we start work in the morning. We want a partner with whom we can take on the world and build something wildly successful. We want to give and receive massages. We want to grow in spirit and know that we are operating in the Creator's purpose for our lives. We want thought-provoking conversations that arouse our intellect and draw us closer together, and I can't forget that we want mind-blowing sex that leaves us depleted. I want that for every married couple, but as we all know, according to statistics, the lifestyle that some live does not support the ideas expressed earlier. I want us all to understand that whatever we want in terms of life, but more importantly in terms of marriage, must be supported by the way we live. Some synonyms for lifestyle are behavior, conduct, habits, style of living, and a way of acting. All the previous attributes when carried out originate on the inside. In other words, what we produce on the outside is a reflection of who we are on the inside. It's an inside job, meaning that we must work on ourselves in order to achieve what we say we want from our marriage. What does your lifestyle say about you or about your marriage?

If what you want in terms of your relationship and what you are getting right now are not in alignment, don't look to anyone to blame or fix it. Look in the mirror! You must be able to take ownership of your situation. Yep, I get it. Some of you are saying right now, "It's not my fault though!" That may be true, and it may not be your fault, but it is indeed your responsibility. If there is a conversation that needs to take place, initiate it. If there is something that you want your spouse to do for you, then you do it first. If you know that you need therapy, get a therapist. TAKE OWNERSHIP! It's amazing to me how much people want to declare how grown they are, but when it comes to actually being grown when difficulties show up, and they have to communicate and do the "work," they miss the mark every time. It is so much easier to point fingers, blame others, and be defensive. As long as you operate in that place, you never will experience the marriage that you desire. Anything worth having will be tested. How will you fare when you are tested? Your mindset, your behavior, your conduct, your habits, your style of living, and the way you act must all create an environment that facilitates what you desire from marriage. If what you are doing right now is not in alignment with what you want, then bind it up and throw it overboard. It cannot go with you on the journey.

Faith and I remember a number of years ago, some friends of ours came to spend the weekend with us. We were living in the city at the time, so we decided to take a walk through the city. Prior to leaving, we decided to have a little coffee before we left. I proceeded to make the coffee, and as customary, I brought Faith a cup. I would have poured some for the other couple, but I wasn't sure how they liked their coffee. I just kind of instructed them to where I put their mugs on the counter and where the cream and sugar was. If I knew what was going to happen next, I would have asked them how they liked their coffee and poured it myself. The husband simply asked his wife, "Babe, can you pour me a cup of coffee while I put my sneakers on?" She responded with a little sass, "No, you can get your own coffee." Faith and I gave each other a quick look. Of course, as friends, we discussed it later, and we poured into the couple. What I know is that they both wanted a loving marriage. They both wanted a pleasant relationship, but their actions were not creating what they desired. Remember, it's not what we face but how we face it. No one is going to hand you a phenomenal marriage. NO ONE! You can't go to Walmart and ask, "On what aisle is your phenomenal marriage?" You can't go online and order it from Amazon. They simply don't have it because it cannot be bought, and Amazon has everything! You must work and build and maintain it for yourself. However, I must warn you that no matter how lovely you think your marriage is or how wonderful your idea is of what you built, IT. MUST. BE. TESTED! The problem is too many individuals have entered into marriage, but they have not done the inside work, so when the test comes, and they are hit with difficulty, they perpetually not only hurt themselves, but their spouse and children, if there are any present. My first marriage was so indicative of this.

I know who I was supposed to be as a man of God in the community where I lived. I know what I was blessed with, but when the test came, and the arguments pursued, it got really bad, and I failed the test miserably - several times. I failed to the point that the police had to come to the house on a number of occasions. In retrospect, many times I asked myself, *How did I get to that place?* The most crucial part in all our tests is the fact that without the inside work, you never understand or can see the subsequent damage that takes place as a result of that work that needed to be done. Did I do it all on my own? No. However, I was a willing participant every time simply because I had not done the inside work.

It's never about the fruit; it is always about the root. You don't plant apple seeds and get an orange tree. Whatever you plant represents the fruit you will bear. Take inventory of your mindset, your behaviors, your conduct, your habits, your style of living, and your way of acting. If they are not consistent with what you want in terms of your marriage, then it's time to make some adjustments. It's time to do the inside work.

The relationship you are in must stand the test of time. Remember, we are talking about a lifetime. If that be the case, it must be sustained and maintained through lifestyle. There are those who are healthy and in shape well into their years because of one thing...LIFESTYLE! There are some who never fall victim to certain temptations because of their lifestyle. There are some who succeed in particular areas because of the lifestyle that they have developed. If you want a marriage that will stand the test of time, what mindset, behavior, conduct, habits, style of living, and\or way of acting are you cultivating? If it is not in alignment with what you always thought about in terms of your marriage, then STOP! Refocus and recalibrate who you are and watch your marriage be transformed. Develop your lifestyle!

CHALLENGE:

TAKE INVENTORY OF YOUR MINDSET, BEHAVIOR, CONDUCT, habits, style of living, way of acting, and your thoughts. Are they consistent or in alignment with what you desire with and from your spouse? If they are not, what services(program, coach, or system) do you need to employ to remove the old attributes that work against you and your marriage and implement the ones that work for you and win?

CHAPTER

ELEVEN

THEORY VS EXECUTION

"When you want to succeed as bad as you want to breathe, then you will be successful."

Dr. Eric Thomas, PhD

M y good friend and brother, Dr. Eric Thomas, - as some call him, ET the Hip Hop Preacher - conducted our premarital coaching as well as presided over our wedding ceremony when we got married in Punta Cana, D.R. I honor and cherish our relationship for a number of reasons but mostly for the fact that he assisted not only in my personal growth but also in my growth as it relates to marriage. Through our brotherhood, I have had the opportunity to have countless conversations and observe him and Dede (his wife) in public as well as in private settings navigate through life as a couple. He is a huge advocate and indeed a practitioner in the area of execution. He is not a fan of just "talking the talk." He consistently emphasizes and demonstrates through his own life "walking the walk." Anything that must come to fruition will not be done only through talking about it. There is some level of execution that must take place. According to him, "Ideas are rewarded, but execution is worshiped," and so it is in marriage. If we are to establish a lifestyle by which we can live, talking about what you are going to do versus actually doing it makes all the difference. The reason why some of us cannot get buy-in from our spouse when it comes to our ideas is simply because when we talk about the things we want to accomplish, there has never been any evidence of what we expressed. When we are creating a lifestyle for our marriage, we must be evidence producers of what we desire. If I tell Faith that I love her, but I never show her my feelings in tangible ways, her belief in my love would dwindle slowly. Why? My love should produce some kind of action. Some may be reading this and saying, "I already know this," and for some of you, you are absolutely correct. You do know this. The question is, "Have you applied what you already know? If you know it, but you have not applied it, it's just as good as not knowing it at all. If you don't know, then get a book, attend a conference, or join a marriage community, workshop, or seminar, but by all means, get the information and then apply it.

It is very interesting to me when we conduct conferences, only one or two people raise their hands when I throw the question out to everyone, "By a show of hands, for a million dollars, is anyone willing to jump out of a plane without a parachute?" I then up the ante, and say, "Ok, for 10 million dollars, is there anyone, by a show of hands willing to jump out of a plane without a parachute?" I usually get maybe one more hand. Now, we are talking about a room on average of about 200-500 people, and only 2 or 3 hands go up when I ask these questions. I usually make my final offer, "By show of hands, I will give 1 billion dollars to the person who will jump out of an airplane without a parachute!" It is at that point that I reveal that they lost out on one billion dollars because the plane is on the ground. The room usually ends in loud awes, and people say, "I can't believe I didn't raise my hand." Let's be honest, I don't have a billion dollars to give anyone, but the point I am trying to make is that information applied changes situations. If I had given that little bit of information before asking the question everyone would have been ready, willing, and able to jump based on the information I provided. What am I saying? Talking is good because that's how thoughts, ideas, and dreams are expressed and understood, but they cannot stand alone without execution. Be properly informed. Make a decision and then execute. Choosing not to do anything is also a decision, but trust me, you do not want to harvest the fruits of indecisiveness.

Michael Jordan in my opinion is hands down the greatest to ever play the game of basketball, and many will agree. Now, some will say Kobe or LeBron is the greatest player to play the game of basketball. How can they feel that way? I don't know but I'm praying for you. The thing I love the most about Jordan is the fact that he "knew" and had an intimate relationship with the game of basketball. The question is, however, no matter how well he knew the game, would he be considered the g.o.a.t. if he didn't execute the way he did? It was the way he showed up every night. It was the hundreds if not thousands of jump shots and foul shots he shot every day. It was the performance in game 5 of the 1997 NBA Finals when he had 7 rebounds, 5 assists, 3 steals, and 1 block in the first 44 minutes. In the second quarter, he scored 17 points, and he scored 15 points in the fourth quarter including a clutch 3-pointer off a pass from Scottie Pippen. He did it while being hammered the entire game by the flu. Plainly put, HE EXECUTED!

Divorce is something that has run rampant through the last 3 generations of my family. As long as I have been alive, I have never seen my grandmother in a real relationship with any man. As a matter of fact, my parents were divorced when I was in the second grade. While we are on the topic, I tried to outrun it, and it also became my reality. I was married in 2003, and I became divorced in 2005. I sometimes laugh at myself simply because I am a marriage coach. How funny is that? The thing I made an absolute mess of is the very field in which I work. According to my track record and statistics, I should be nowhere close to this field of work, but the defining difference is relative to two things: 1. Your past does not have to be your present or your future. 2. I received information that allowed me to make better decisions specifically in the area of relationships. My first marriage ended in 2005. I was married to Faith in June of 2011, and we have been rocking strong ever since because of information, a decision based on that information, and execution.

It is never good to move through life not being informed. Ignorant decisions can cost you more than you know. Even if you are amongst the informed, you must do something with the information you have. There are 3 types of people in this world: those who don't know what to do, and those people are confused. There are those who know what to do and don't do it, and those people are frustrated. Then, there is the last group - those who know what to do and do it, and those people are fulfilled. Don't you want to be fulfilled? What is stopping you from doing that which you know you should do? In chapter 4, I spoke about the mantra, "Enter to learn, depart to serve," because I believe it personifies this chapter. What will you learn about your marriage, about your thoughts, or about your mindset that you will use to make yourself better for your relationship? What you know in theory MUST be applied.

CHAPTER

TWELVE

GET REPS

"From shaky to good and from good to great, ultimately, what we want are phenomenal marriages, but phenomenal marriages don't just happen. They take work, so let's do that work!"

Quest Green

In case you didn't know, reps are short for repetitions. They are the action of one complete strength exercise like one bicep curl or one bench press. Sets are how many reps you do in a row between periods of rest. By using reps and sets to guide your strength workouts, you can pinpoint and achieve your fitness goals with more control. Getting reps is not a pleasurable experience when you are new to working out or starting out at the gym simply because there is a lot of pain and soreness that for the most part subsides during those periods of rest. However, if you are committed to the process of fitness, not to mention looking great, the rewards are GREAT! I remember when I started my fitness journey with Rochelle T. Parks, the Health Motivator, and a motivator she is! I remember belly aching about my workouts and the pain and the soreness I was enduring, and she replied by saying, "I feel you, BUT you will NEVER achieve your fitness goals unless you pass through the tunnel of pain." When she said that, I had a decision to make. C'mon! She is the health motivator! If you have ever seen my friend Rochelle, she is in her 50's, and I promise you she looks like she is in her mid to late 30's, so she knows exactly what she is talking about. The question is, "Was I going to quit because of the pain, or was I going to be committed to the goal? I chose to be committed to the goal. It is a journey that I am still on, but I have developed so much between that time and now. I am down 30 lbs, And I am looking to take off a couple more. I have built a lot more muscle as well. Now, I'm no body builder, but my wife has said to me on a couple of occasions that I look so much younger. That's enough motivation to step it up a notch.

In the journey of marriage, too many people decide to quit or remain in a gray area because of the challenge, pain, difficulty, or opposition they face. My fitness trainer, Darnyl Allen, used to ask me, "Where are your problem areas? What are the areas that you want to change the most?" After sharing with him the areas in which I wanted to experience change, he would explain that we first must build your secondary muscles in order to support your primary muscles properly, so the change you want to experience will be very noticeable. I was in pain just listening to him! What we were doing together was identifying the areas in which we both knew I was deficient and putting together a plan of execution. His whole modus operandi and slogan for his business is "change over comfort." Was it difficult? Absolutely! What I was doing under his instruction was getting the reps in, and the more sets I did with each training session, the more comfortable I became with the process and the weight. Then, as soon as I got to the place where it was comfortable, he increased the weight...a whole other discussion for another time! What I want you to focus on is the areas in your marriage in which you know as an individual you are not proficient. Do you respond to adverse situations with anger, or do you lash out? Are you defensive when your spouse brings a fault to your attention? Do you punish your spouse by stonewalling, being critical, or holding contempt for them because a discussion or situation didn't go your way? In what area do you need to work? Do you need a coach or a therapist? As awkward or painful as it may feel in the beginning, if you remain committed to the process of becoming better, you will, and your marriage will show the work you've done.

I have a marriage community called the Greenhouse Marriage Community, and one of the thoughts that most couples have that are exposed in one of our marriage community meetings is, "I thought that we were alone?" I want to share with you that you are not alone. There are many marriages that experience the same issues you experience. As a matter of fact ALL MARRIAGES experience issues at some point or another. They are very necessary for growth. As I always say, however, it is not what you face but how you face it. I have known couples who have had opposing feelings and emotions in their relationship who made a joint decision to put their feelings aside and embrace commitment to their vow "for better or worse." It just so happens that this is the time of "worse." There are many people who got married for better or best, and when worse shows up, they want to bail out.

I'd like to remind us that marriage is a LIFETIME commitment that requires you to weather the storms associated with your relationship through commitment. The couple that is able to see the areas in which they are not so proficient go to therapy, get a coach, and sometimes go to conferences or seminars. They make some adjustments and turn those adjustments into a way of life. That is the couple that is destined to thrive in major ways. Too many couples (and most times it's men) say, "Why do I need to go to a therapist?" "Why do I need a marriage coach?" Those professionals are important simply because they have the tools that you need, and they are trained to deal with the issues that keep causing your marriage to fail because of P.R.I.D.E. - Perpetually Repeating Ignorant Decisions Every day! You don't grow your marriage without challenge, difficulty, or opposition. Consistency and commitment should be deemed major parts of your marital relationship. Without them, you will not achieve your marital goals.

CHALLENGE:

IDENTIFY THE AREAS IN YOUR MARRIAGE THAT ARE PAIN POINTS. Don't run from them. Face them head on. Have the difficult conversation. Carry out the difficult deed. Whatever the need is, meet it! NO EXCUSES! Come up with an action plan. Implement it and GET REPS!

PART FOUR

Legacy

CHAPTER
THIRTEEN
LEGACY

"Tell your children of it, and let your children tell their children, and their children to another generation."

Joel 1:3

M y parents got a divorce when I was about the age of seven, and I had no idea how that divorce would affect me until I was much older. There were moments in my adulthood when I was angry at them for not trying to work things out or keep our family together. As a child, I was too young to understand my predicament, but as I became an adult and had friends who came from two parent homes, it became more and more evident over the years what I was really missing. To some extent, my development suffered for it, and I looked to find solace in relationships for all the wrong reasons. You can say I was a bit angry, but I never let it show, and I powered through it by saying to myself, "It's all good," even though I knew it wasn't. Moreover, it never really showed on the outside or at least to the untrained eye until I got in that one relationship that almost cost me my sanity and not to mention my freedom. I could see all the warning signs, but the sex was so dope that I either was completely blind to it, or I turned a blind eye to it because I didn't want to mess up my access to the sex. I was married for all the wrong reasons, and because of that, the relationship was tumultuous as ever. The marriage lasted for two years, and when I arrived at the place of divorce, I realized in its entirety, what I had been angry with my parents about. How could I be angry with them though? I did the same thing. You simply cannot give what you don't have, and they simply did not have "it" at the time. My mother was 20 when she had me, and I believe my father was 21 or 22. They decided to get divorced when they were 27 and 28. I'm not sure how I would fare with a baby at their age, not to mention they had my sister at 24 and 25. By the time they got divorced at ages 27 and 28, they had two children while still trying to figure themselves out in a country in which they were neither born nor grew up. Looking back in retrospect and through healed lenses, I neither am no longer low-key angry with my parents nor do I hold them hostage to their old selves. As a matter of fact, outside of them being their own success stories, they are very good friends now even though they are married to other individuals. I will admit though, there are moments when I think, *Why couldn't you do this way back when?* The truth is that they were not back then who they are now. I'm just glad that they can be friends. I want to share with you that foundation and legacy are very important. As a matter of fact, they are everything! I started on what would be a 6-year journey in making a better foundation for myself, my wife, and family to be. I stopped going to the clubs I would frequent. I stopped hanging with my normal crowd. I would read books on self-development. I started going to church more and reading my Bible more. I started being in the company of people who were in the places and spaces that I was not to help me become a better individual because I realized that if I was ever to do this thing called marriage again, I not only wanted to be better, but also I wanted to be able to make better decisions including picking a wife.

It is very important that you understand once you become married you - whether you realize it or not - become an immediate reference point as either what to do or what not to do in a relationship. Be mindful of what you exhibit to others and more importantly to your children.

Faith and I remind ourselves from time to time that our marriage is not only about us. It is also about the marriages that our children also will have later on in life. It's about every other marriage that looks at our relationship, and yes, your relationship as a standard. If you think they are not watching, trust me, they are!

My son Nico is pretty much my personal copycat. Everything I do he wants to do. I've said some things in a public setting that were not necessarily bad words, but he overheard the conversation in which I was engaged with other adults, and he heard some things that really only adults can say. He has made the mistake of repeating those things which prompted me to have a little father-son talk with him on the differences between being an adult and being a child. Of course, in our conversation, he always says, "Daddy, can I ask you a question?" Of course, my answer is always yes. He then asks, "How come you get to say those things, but I can't?" Now, in my day, if you asked your parents that sort of question as a child, you might end up on the emergency room table at the local hospital. However, I can see that he is trying to understand, and when you think about it, it really is a legit question. What I am saying doesn't have any bad words in it. In his mind, he's thinking, *Why can't I say them as well?* I really considered this question, and I came to the conclusion that in his efforts to be like me, he wants to go where I go, do what I do, and say what I say. It probably would be in my best interest and his to be careful about what I show him. Am I saying to be fake? Absolutely not. However, I realized that he does not understand all the nuances of being an adult, so I must be responsible for him. Some of us need to break negative cycles that may have started with our own upbringing in order to launch a new legacy for the next generation.

Within the realm of marriage, as in life, we must remember to be very mindful of what we show family, our children, and yes, others. Our actions, thoughts, behaviors, and the way we choose to use them have long lasting effects on the generations behind us. We are building our legacy by design and not by default.

The privilege of being married and being called a leader are very powerful things because you have the ability to shape hearts and influence minds simply by co-existing. You have heard it said that with great power comes great responsibility. To be married is a powerful thing on a number of fronts. It's too bad that many who are married don't understand the influence and power they have, and they are thereby reckless. If you are married and reading this, I want to declare to you that you are powerful. Look at what it says in Matthew 18:19. "Again, I say unto you that if two of you shall agree on earth concerning ANYTHING that they shall ask, it shall be done for them by My Father who is in Heaven." READ IT AGAIN! Do you see why He says to be fruitful, multiply, subdue the Earth and have dominion? There is no time to be at odds with one another. Do you need healing? GET IT! Do you have a vision for your relationship? You should! Why? There are much more important things at stake. As my brother, E.T., would say, "GREATNESS IS UPON YOU!" What is your marriage saying to people and the next generation? I'd like to share with you a term in corporate America known as corporate responsibility (CR). It is basically about the impact an organization makes on society, the environment, and the economy. Having an effective CR program within a company contributes positively to all stakeholders as well as adds value for the organization itself, and it ensures that the organization operates in a sustainable way.

WORK:

1. How are you operating in, if I may say, "marital responsibility?"
2. What kind of impact are you making on your spouse and those around you from a marital standpoint?

3. Are you contributing effectively to your spouse and the relationship?
4. Are you adding VALUE to your spouse and the relationship?
5. Are you operating in your relationship in a sustainable way?

THINK ABOUT THESE THINGS. LEGACY IS DEPENDING ON YOU. What will you do for it?

CHAPTER
FOURTEEN
LEAVE AN INHERITANCE

"A good man leaves an inheritance to his children..."

Proverbs 13:22

When we speak of inheritance, we have a tendency to think about money or some monetary attribute, and while I want to leave money for my children, to do so without giving them principles, practices, and wisdom while they develop understanding could be catastrophic. Plus, that is not what the fullness of inheritance is all about. The word, "inheritance," is defined as: the reception of genetic qualities by transmission from parent to offspring, or the acquisition of a possession, condition or trait from past generations. The Scriptures tell us that what we do today directly influences the cycle of family traits, beliefs, and actions - good or bad - for generations to come. Amongst a plethora of things pertaining to life, my parents gave me what they had in terms of relationship and how it works. I learned from watching their inner workings and not so much from conversations that necessarily dealt with relationships. They handled divorce the way they did because of the information they had and the things to which they were exposed. I constantly am working on myself because I want to leave an inheritance to my children and children's children, so I can show them:

1. Marriage is the most important decision they ever will make outside their decision to follow Christ.
2. Marriage is a beautiful institution marked with mountain high as well as valley low experiences that can have the greatest of rewards, providing that you remain committed to each other and the relationship.
3. You cannot give to your children, but more importantly to your spouse, what you do not have. If you don't have it, and your relationship needs it, then identify what "it" is, embrace it, and develop it.

Even though I am proficient in the things stated above, there are still those moments when I fall short and become so frustrated and disappointed with myself that I have to go back and make explanations and apologies for my behavior.

I want to share with some of you reading this that I don't expect you to achieve these things overnight, but I do expect you to work on them constantly in every aspect of your life. Remember, it's an inside job! In order to leave something worthwhile to your next generation, you must develop who you are in all areas of your life.

I have to work twice as hard now on my relationship than I ever did before. Why? Outside the fact that I am on my second, and yes final marriage, my daughter Zoey lives with me, and she's been living with me since she was 14. She is now 20, and I have had the awesome privilege of getting to show her something different than what she is accustomed to seeing. Unfortunately, because of my decision to divorce her mom, that now makes her a product of that same divorce. My time is limited as to what I need to show her, not to mention the conversations we need to have prior to her going out into the world on her own, and here's what's difficult. I have to wait for the right time to have those conversations because sometimes, she is not ready, or she just doesn't want to have them right now, which teaches me also that there is a time, place, space, and season for everything under the sun. She constantly is watching Faith and me, whether we believe it or not. I know this because of some of the comments she has made as it relates to us. Even when Faith and I are not seeing eye to eye, my children see that as well. They get an opportunity to see what it looks like when difficulties arise, and they see how we handle them and keep the relationship intact. Now, they are not privy to behind-the-door conversations, but because of our personal inside work, they never hear or see reckless shouting, name calling, or any behavior that would have an adverse effect on their view of marriage and relationships.

Faith and I randomly hug one another in our home. We randomly kiss one another, and I even rub on her booty every now and then. LOL. The kids, especially Zoey, play like they're gagging and getting ready to throw up when they see us express our feelings for one another, but whether they realize it or not, we are loving on one another in a genuine way, and we also are reenforcing what we teach them in terms of having healthy relationships.

There are many things that you can leave as an inheritance, but the best thing you can leave for your children is the way you love your spouse. Marriage is the cornerstone of a healthy civilization. It is the cornerstone of a neighborhood. Look at the effects through statistics of what happens when a marriage falls apart. They are staggering not only to the two involved but also to the children if there are any in the relationship. Statistics regularly show that when marriages fall apart, homes fall apart. If homes fall apart, neighborhoods fall apart. If neighborhoods fall apart, cities fall apart. If cities fall apart, states fall apart. Do you see where I am going with this? Am I saying that a child cannot be raised by a single parent? Absolutely not! However, I am saying two parents are better than one parent. There are some things that a father brings to the equation of family that a mother doesn't, and there are some things that a mother brings that a father doesn't. When these elements are combined in the home, it is extremely beneficial, not only to the child but to the generations to come beyond that child.

Look at the statistics. The Kids Count Data Center for The Annie E. Casey Foundation compiled data acquired from the Population Reference Bureau's analysis data from the U.S. Census Bureau and Supplementary Survey 2002 through 2019. They stated, "Children growing up in single-parent families typically do not have the same economic or human resources available as those growing up in two-parent families. Compared with children in married-couple families, children raised in single-parent households are more likely to drop out of school, to have or cause a teen pregnancy, and to experience a divorce in adulthood." WHOA! Talk about information changing situations! Do I have to explain to you why my attitude is the way that it is towards marriage? Why am I passionate about it the way that I am? Divorce directly affects our generations to come. PERIOD! Let me provide you some hope, however, with some flip side research. According to the Urban Institute, "Families play a central role in shaping the well-being of children and adults; they are a safety net and the primary investor in the next generation." Do you know what is at the foundation of those families? You guessed it! Healthy marriages. Therefore, in essence, if marriages fall apart, homes fall apart and so on. Moreover, the inverse also must be true. If marriages stay together and work, then homes stay together, and neighborhoods, cities, states stay together for GENERATIONS to come.

If inheritance is qualities transmitted to our offspring, let a part of that inheritance that we leave for them be the love for our spouses that will serve as firm foundations for our families for years, decades, and should God delay his coming, for centuries to come.

WORK:

1. How are your daily actions in your treatment of your spouse affecting your generations to come?
2. Where do you need to embrace an idea or mindset that is in alignment with your marriage?
3. Which ones do you need to let go that are not in alignment with your marriage?
4. Create an accountability system with your spouse or someone you trust that will assist you in making these changes.

CHAPTER
FIFTEEN

THE LIGHT: YOUR MARRIAGE AS A REFERENCE POINT

"Let your light so shine before men that they may see your good works and glorify your Father which is in heaven."

Matthew 5:16

W e are definitely in a dark place as it relates to marriage. People treat it as some arrangement you become a part of, and if things don't pan out the way you want, then they bail out. That was never the basis for marriage. Throughout this entire book, if you never get anything else, please embrace the fact that marriage is supposed to grow you and change you for the better. Every difficult moment, every challenging situation, every opposition faced, and every difficulty experienced is an indication of the area in which you need to grow. If your response to the mood, moment, or situation is one of contempt for the other person, one of stubbornness, or one of any other negative response that is counterproductive to a positive outcome, then this is your area for growth. Remember, it's not what you face in marriage. It's how you face it. If you always choose to look at your difficult and challenging situations through the lens of growth, then you will do just that—grow.

I have said it in multiple chapters in this book. IT IS AN INSIDE JOB!

How would I look if I talked crazy to Faith or devalued her? If I mistreated her? If I took her for granted? More importantly, what kind of effect would I have on another couple who witnessed that kind of interaction? What effect would I have on my children if they were witnesses to that kind of behavior? When Zoey started college, she attended school locally. Before she got her car, I would take her to her classes and wait until she entered the building. Then, I would drive off. Her classes were in the main building on campus, and the entire front of the building was made of that 2-way mirror kind of glass where you couldn't see in from the outside, but you could see out from the inside. There was a lady who sat at an administration desk just inside the entry of the building, and unbeknownst to me, she was watching us for about a month. One day she decided to stop Zoey and say, "Sweetheart, is that your dad?" Zoey responded, "Yes ma'am. It is." She began to tell Zoey, "Honey, you have a great dad. I watch him drop you off every time you have classes, and he NEVER leaves until you walk into the building." If people are watching you when you operate individually, imagine what happens when two people come together for the purpose of marriage?

I am the first generation born in the United States. Everyone else before me either was born and raised in Jamaica or Guyana. I make mention of that to say that the West Indian culture is still very strong with me. The game of Dominoes is one of the great pastimes for numerous West Indian men, and prior to getting married, we would play dominoes until 2, 3, 4:00 a.m., and sometimes, we would play until the sun came up. What can I say? We love dominoes! I don't play as often as I used to play, not because I don't want to, but there are greater demands on my life in this season of marriage and family. However, I still do play occasionally. Recently the fellas got together to play Dominoes, and as usual we were having a great time chilling with one another, talking smack on the Dominoes table, and so on. I happened to look down at my watch and saw that it was about 1:40 a.m., so I finished my game, began to say goodbye to everyone, and proceeded to make my exit. As I was leaving, one of the gents I met a couple of months back said, "Q, every time we get together, you leave around 2:00 a.m. That must be your curfew time." Some of the brothers who have known me a lot longer said, "Q, we already know what it is," and I replied to the gentleman by saying, "It's not that, but it is that." Now, there were many different dynamics going on in that small exchange. First, it's just a little clowning. No, harm done. Secondly, I also know, however, that there is truth in a pun. Now, I am grown, not only in age, but also in my thinking. I have nothing to prove to anyone other than God and the person with whom I am doing life, and that is Faith. She usually expects me to come in around that time when I do decide to go play Dominoes, and I want to keep it that way. Why? I do not want to create any insecurities for her or in our relationship. I personally like peace in my relationship. There is nothing like it! It can be achieved easily when you are not only considering yourself. Some of you are not experiencing the peace and harmony that you should in your relationship because you are only thinking about yourself. I know because that used to be me at one time. The difference is that I began to see quickly that my old ideology was not working for me. It was working against me and my relationship. When that happens, you have a decision to make. You can make adjustments or remain stagnant. I decided to make the adjustments. The natural result is growth and peace. You cannot be a man and a child at the same time. You must choose which one you want to be and act accordingly.

I never knew that this particular individual was watching my movements. Whatever he saw affected him enough to speak on it. I also know, however, without even paying attention, the work that you put in when no one is watching, and the adjustments that you make for the enhancement of the relationship, show when they are watching and pricks them to a level of conviction without you even having to say a word. What is my point? They always are watching, especially the moment you become a married couple. What does your marriage (light) do? Does it shine and give light to others, or is it one that burns down everything around it? Sometimes, we can be tempted to think that our marriage is only about us. That is far from reality, whether you like it or not. However, I would hope that it gives light to others. The truth is that if no one is coming to ask you "how to" questions on marriage, you may need to reevaluate if you are doing marriage correctly.

It's your time now. It's time for you to decide where you want to go on this journey of marriage. The mandate is and always has been to be fruitful, multiply, subdue the Earth, and have dominion. It's achievable! More importantly, you deserve it! You can't buy it in a store, but it does come at a cost. That cost is called WORK! What adjustments are you willing to make? What mindsets are you willing to change? What conversations with your spouse are you willing to have? It's waiting on you! My prayer is that you will make the decision and make it now.

When that is the philosophy that you cultivate, it shows on the outside. In the most difficult times, people watch you to see what your response is going to be, and if you respond adversely while others are watching you, you have affected their outlook on relationships in a negative kind of way. The bond that you share with your spouse is so much bigger than the two of you. Therefore, this is your opportunity. Take the journey to have the marriage you always wanted, and I'll see you at phenomenal.

EPILOGUE

N ow that you have reached the end of this book, you should have some tools and focus areas as you take the journey to a phenomenal marriage. Information applied changes situations, and while there is no way for us to put ALL the information in one book, you should have exactly what you need to start or continue the journey.

The following is a summary of the focus and concepts of this book. They will help you on your exploration.

Chapter 1: FOUNDATION: This chapter introduces the first of the 4 pillars and helps you to understand the fundamentals of a relationship and understand the love, commitment, and mindset necessary to navigate the relationship when difficult challenges arise..

Chapter 2: FOUNDATION Part Deux: This chapter is a continuation of chapter 1. Basically, it takes you through how the challenges of

Chapter 1 look, as well as it helps you understand the idea of commitment and ways you can work together and not against each other to solve issues.

Chapter 3: KNOW THE CREATOR: This chapter helps you completely embrace the idea that marriage is a spiritual institution created by God, and a personal relationship with Him has huge benefits for your marriage.

Chapter 4: WHO DO I NEED TO BE?: Learn how the institution of marriage is one of servitude and discover ways to achieve the mindset and practices necessary to be successful in marriage while eliminating the ones that work against you.

Chapter 5: LAY THE FOUNDATIONS FOR BUILDING: Understand that phenomenal marriages are created by design and not by default. As you begin your journey to a phenomenal marriage, formulate a strategic plan on how you want your marriage to look.

Chapter 6: LOVE: This is the introduction to the second of the 4 pillars, and it helps you learn the importance of enjoying your marriage. Learn to make deposits into your marriage on a regular basis, especially for the days you will need to make a withdrawal.

Chapter 7: LOVE DON'T ALWAYS FEEL GOOD: Learn how to embrace the moments of love that don't feel so good. One major part of achieving a phenomenal marriage is being able to receive rebuke from your spouse when necessary.

Chapter 8: WHAT DOES LOVE REQUIRE OF ME?: Gain clarity on the fact that marriage is work! The rewards far exceed the work, but you must work to maintain it. It requires a version of you that you currently are not, but achieving that version is inclusive of the work.

Chapter 9: HOW TO LOVE MY SPOUSE: Gain clarity on who your spouse is as an individual and what lights their fire. This chapter highlights methods to love them the way they want to be loved and not how you receive love.

Chapter 10: LIFESTYLE: This is the introduction to the third of the 4 pillars, and it focuses on the environment you create for your marriage. Whatever you plant in your marriage is what it will produce.

Chapter 11: THEORY vs EXECUTION: Operate beyond good intentions. Marriage is significantly more than having good thoughts towards your spouse or expressing in words what you feel toward your spouse. Your words must be manifested through action.

Chapter 12: GET REPS: Embrace the mindset that the practices that benefit the relationship in marriage is not a one-time thing. It must be carried out on a regular basis in order to build the strength of the relationship.

Chapter 13: LEGACY: This is the introduction to the fourth and final pillar - legacy. Gain clarity on the idea that once you say, "I do," your marriage is not only about you. You are now a focal point for your children and everyone else who desires marriage.

Chapter 14: LEAVE AN INHERITANCE: Understand the Biblical principle about leaving an inheritance for your children and recognize that it is not only associated with money. Embrace the idea that the principles of your marriage must be carried through the generations after you.

Chapter 15: THE LIGHT: Learn how to conduct your relationship in a way that is inspiring to those around you. Embrace the idea that your marriage should be a light in a world of darkness.

THE TIME IS NOW! YOU HAVE EXACTLY WHAT YOU NEED IN order to take action and make your marriage phenomenal. Your spouse is depending on you. Your children are depending on you. Your grandchildren are depending on you, and generations to come are depending on you. What you do now not only affects your current relationship, but your actions affect generations to come. Be ye cognizant and execute! From shaky to good and from good to great, ultimately, what we want are phenomenal marriages, but phenomenal marriages don't just happen. They take work! Let's do that WORK, and I'll see you at phenomenal!

ABOUT THE AUTHOR

Quest Green is currently the CEO of The Greenhouse - a company dedicated to the development and preservation of marriages. He is also the co-host alongside L. David Harris of the "Marriage Ain't for SuckaZ" podcast - podcast developed in a movement to support couples in their marital success. Whether recording a weekly podcast, conducting a *Greenhouse* marriage conference or a church seminar or creating new marriage content, Quest has the ability to reach husbands and wives and give them hope and courage to make the necessary adjustments that allow both spouses to achieve the love they deserve and desire. After suffering a divorce in 2005, Quest knows all about the importance of core values and the role they play in choosing the "right spouse." He went from experiencing the effects of an unpleasant divorce to being remarried in 2011 and building a family with his wife, Faith, their daughter Zoey (from his previous marriage), and their sons, Dominic (Nico) and Mason.

Quest's personal pursuit of being a better husband and father has led him to not only become a professional marriage coach, but also he is a graduate of the University of North Carolina Charlotte. He and his family happily reside in Charlotte, North Carolina. Most importantly, Quest wants spouses to know that no matter where they are in the spectrum from shaky to good or from good to great, ultimately, they want to have Phenomenal Marriages, but Phenomenal Marriages don't just happen. They take work! If he can do it, SO CAN YOU!

ACKNOWLEDGMENTS

Sometimes, we would like to think that the accomplishments we have made are on our own. Even if that is the case for some, that has never been the case for me. It always has been about the Tribe! I am humbled and honored by everyone I ever met who contributed to my development in any way, shape, or form. I promise to continue to make you proud.

Thank you to Jasmine Womack and your entire team. I got this book done because you gave me the blueprint. Coach Joel Boyce, you da man. God bless yall. Thank you to everyone who played a role in my development, spiritually and otherwise. To my family at the East New York SDA Church in Brooklyn, NY, you produced me and raised me. To the former Springfield Gardens SDA Church, - currently the Community Worship Center in Queens, NY, - you gave me "family" that I will have for the rest of my life. To the Nieves Family, the Hunt Family, the Sylvester family, the Markes family, the Pilgrim Family, thank you! Hanson

Place Elementary, Excelsior Elementary, Greater New York Academy.

Thank you to my New York Family Uingston "Mikey" Markes and Curtis Pilgrim; desires and endeavors may have separated us in flesh but never in spirit. Keith Mitchell, Victor Brochet, Paul "PJ" Best, Brian "Pharoah" Johnson, Mike Prentice, Fabian Lawla, Jules Hutson, Zaneta Williams, Warren and Mayna Thomas, Roger and Lynette Thomas, Karen Pilgrim, Patrick and Paul Graham, John Lazarus, Heather Lyons, Andre Lyons, The Ashmead Family, Yolanda Nieves, Wendy Nieves, Naja Hunt, Daryl Hunt, Antonio Pilgrim, Andre Sylvester, Wendell Sylvester, Robert Sylvester, Paul Patrick and Gary Graham, Oliver Gittens, Rhonda Gittens, Carl Scott, Pastor Clark, Pastor Laffit Cortes

To A Tribe Called Quest, Kamaal Fareed (Q-tip), Ali Shaheed Muhammed, Jarobi White my brother you already know. To you and your lovely bride, Danielle, thank you for your love and support. To Deisha Taylor, I am your brother for life. To Malik Izzak Taylor (Phife), I got to see the world because of you. I miss you terribly and can't wait to see you again. RIP, Estelle thank you.

My Atlanta family, The WHOLE West End SDA Church family, you will always be my church home. Pastor Calvin Preston, Pastor Daryl Shon Anderson, Aneitra Jones, Ashante Tucker, Marshall Fox, Rochelle T. Parks, Dion Liverpool, Keisha Russell, Crystal Russell. Julian, Neil, and Kevin Davis my brothers forever. Jeffrey and Joy Walker and Jewell Ralph, yuh done know. The Jimmerson Family (Momma Ruby, Chandra, Dede). Gil Francois, Stephen Simmons, Imani Malikini, Meme Williams, Ryan and Sherri Manning, Michelle and Will Shaw, Madison and Doreen

Wisdom, Aaron and Tia Miller, The Taffe Family, Kevin Taffe, Michael Lewis, Maurice Taffe, Jason and Devaki Youngblood, Charles and Simone Arrington, you both are the epitome of love.

My Marriage Book Club Family, Will and Tameka Green, Marc and Drea Houston, Ty and Sookie White, Mark and Von Blakely, Anthony and Kenya Odom, Craig and Tiffany Bell, Shelton and Natasha Jefferies, Eric and Vi King, Tim and Tonya Longmire, thank you for your love, comradery, and for holding me accountable and causing me to grow consistently.

My Brothers: Eric Thomas you have always been my friend, my brother, and many times my Pastor. I hope you understand the fullness when I say, "Thank You."

Dede Mosely, I know you are not a brother, but I can't mention E without you. Big Sis, you have affected Faith and my life and sometimes without even having to say a word, Thank You!

Demetrius Flowers, Jeremy Anderson, Ryan Manning, Jon Samon, Lee Lamb, Joey Kibble, Derrick Williams, John Jimmerson, David Troffort, Chris Crumpler, Dr. Ty Douglas, Derrick Green, Tyrone Green, Derrick Green, Lorenzo Prater, Brian "BK" Keith, Paul "Preech" Garrett, Karl Phillips, Jamel Jackson, Joseph Wilson, Darrell Palmes, Eddie Butler, Mason West, LaDon Daniels, Carlas "CJ" Quinney, Jemal King, Burks "Skip to my Lou" Holland, Greg Arneaud, Jamel Jackson, Jamie Cook, Inky Johnson, Demetrius Flowers, Walter Bivens, Kevin Davis, Shannon Austin, Dewane Mutunga, Marshall Fox, Mostafa Ghonim.

To My Greenhouse Community: Tim and Shawnda Morris, love yall to no ends! Keila and Jorge Sierra, Joel and Ciara Montoya, Lemoine and Crystal Robinson, Clive and Vernetta Alonzo, Vince and Angela Parker, Van and Carolyn Flowers, Cody and Kiara Hall, Ken and Tiffany Hayes, Michael and Rochelle T. Parks, Kali and Sonovia Harmon, Donte and Abriana Carter, Eric and Adriane Adkins, Anthony and Stephanie Williams, Chrystina and Ryan McGriff, Jason and Corisma Johnson, Tina and Joey Kibble, Randall and Curtisha Cook, Patrick and Gwen Pete, Emmasara and Clint Mcmillion. Eva Palacios, Ray and Tanya Keffer. Let's change the marriage world!

Charlotte Family: To The Entire Trinity Worship Center Family under the leadership of Pastor Daniel Kelly, brother, you are doing a fantastic job. I am fed weekly by you! Patrick and Carla Jones, Daren and Gloria Smith, Marc and Michelle Cooper, Jeff and Cassie Phipps, David and Mary Howard, Aaron and Lisa Jones, Anthony and Katrina Heath, Monica and Eric Lamb.

Men of my Life: My Dad, John Green Sr., this season of our relationship is priceless. I love and thank you for giving me life. Winston "Pop" Green (my stepfather), when God made you, He broke the mold. They don't make 'em like you any more.

Thank you to my Family: To my mother, Audrey Green, I don't know where to start or end. You are the consummate mother. Thank you for giving me life! To Elizabeth Ramos-Green(my stepmother) your nurturing is unmatched. Thank you for being my second mother. Lorne and Roneka Green, Gavril Green, Latifah Green, Sandra Kay Brown (Auntie Kippy), Michelle Cuthbert, Chris Cuthbert.

Gone but never forgotten: Barbara Robertshaw, Grandma I miss you so much. I wish you were still here, but

God's plan is perfect! Grandpa Leonard Green, Grandma Daisy Green, every time I sat with you you gave me stories about me that I could never remember. Uncle David Green, Uncle Joseph "Doodie" Green, Jeanette Cuthbert, Uncle Carl Green, Uncle Charlie Green, Will Palacios.

To everyone who has ever been a client of mine, bought a piece of merch, listened to a podcast, come to a conference, followed me on Instagram, TikTok, Facebook, or Youtube, watched or shared my videos, or supported me from the heart with words and kind gestures, Thank you, Thank You Thank You!

I could not possibly remember everyone… If I forgot you, please charge it to my head and not my heart.

To my wife and love of my life, Faith, thank you for simply being yourself. God knew what He was doing when he presented you in high school. Who knew that we would be doing life together and loving it! I will continue to work until every dream is fulfilled or until God says for me to rest.

To Zoey, Dominic (Nico), and Mason, it gives me joy to be called "Father" by you. I know I can be a bit "much," but you'll see why in due time. You are the best kids in the world!

God, where would I be without you? Like my left arm, I'd never be right. I give you all glory for this…

With Gratefulness,
Quest